COOKIES *for* EVERYONE

COOKIES *for* EVERYONE

99 *Deliciously Customizable Bakeshop Recipes*

MIMI COUNCIL

LIFE
LONG

Da Capo Press

Hachette Book Group

1290 Avenue of the Americas, New York, NY 10104

HachetteBooks.com

Twitter.com/HachetteBooks

Instagram.com/HachetteBooks

Printed in the United States of America

First Edition: November 2019

Published by Da Capo Press, an imprint of Perseus Books, LLC, a subsidiary of Hachette Book Group, Inc. The Da Capo Press name and logo is a trademark of the Hachette Book Group.

The publisher is not responsible for websites (or their content) that are not owned by the publisher.

Print book interior design by Lorie Pagnozzi

Library of Congress Cataloging-in-Publication Data

Names: Council, Mimi, author.

Title: Cookies for everyone: 99 deliciously customizable bakeshop recipes / by Mimi Council.

Description: First edition. | New York, NY: Da Capo Press, an imprint of Perseus Books, LLC, 2019. | Includes bibliographical references and index.

Identifiers: LCCN 2019002116| ISBN 9780738285610 (paper over board: alk. paper) | ISBN 9780738285603 (ebook: alk. paper)

Subjects: LCSH: Cookies. | LCGFT: Cookbooks.

Classification: LCC TX772 .C662 2019 | DDC 641.86/54—dc23

LC record available at https://lccn.loc.gov/2019002116

ISBNs: 978-0-7382-8561-0 (hardcover), 978-0-7382-8560-3 (ebook)

LSC-C

10 9 8 7 6 5 4 3 2 1

CONTENTS

INTRODUCTION: ONE SMART COOKIE

MY NAME IS MIMI AND I'VE NEVER MET A COOKIE I DIDN'T LIKE. As far back as I can remember, I've been sneaking, eating, snacking on, baking, and creating cookies. When I was growing up, cookies were a forbidden treat and that's probably why I've always been so obsessed—I never knew when I'd get my next cookie fix. Even as I've gotten older and know I can eat cookies daily (which I do), the little kid inside me is worried I might not get one. So I turned my passion and obsession into my business. I make sure everyone has the opportunity to get their cookie fix by stopping by my bakery, Dessert'D Organic Bake Shop.

I started baking cookies as soon as I was old enough to follow a recipe. To be honest, it was all part of my master plan to eat more cookies. My mom didn't allow a lot of sweets in our house, and there were strict rules about when we could and couldn't eat desserts. If we were hungry and it wasn't time for a meal, we were encouraged to eat healthy snacks like fruits and vegetables, string cheese, or a glass of milk. We always had healthy meals, and my mom cooked them from scratch every night. That means she was in the kitchen a lot. She encouraged us to help her cook, because she felt that if we were in the kitchen we were learning something—like how to read, how to follow instructions, and how to create something. That's how I started baking cookies and eating cookies with high-quality ingredients—according to Mom. And so my obsession blossomed.

I continued to bake cookies throughout my teenage years, but when I was seventeen years old I graduated high school early "to live in the mountains and snowboard every day" in lieu of going to college. The day after graduation, I packed my car and moved cross-country from the Midwest to Mammoth Lakes, California. And I took my cookie recipes with me, in a small blue recipe box. Living at eight thousand feet made me quickly learn to adjust my recipes in order to bake them at high altitude so I could continue to enjoy freshly baked cookies.

As time passed, I stopped being a ski bum and got a "real" job at Roxy, an action-sports company, which took me to sea-level Huntington Beach, California. I was working in the industry that I loved, and I was making enough money to stock my kitchen with cookie-baking ingredients at all times. This was when my cookie baking really spiraled out of control. I quickly became known to my friends as Mimi Cookies, because I took them everywhere I went.

Then I was commissioned by a friend to bake cookies for her wedding. She was gluten-free and was having a hard time finding good options. I said yes immediately, even though I had never made gluten-free cookies before. But I thought, how hard could they be? I knew I'd figure it out. I test baked a few batches and let her try them before we settled on a couple of flavors for her wedding. I soon realized I had other friends that were gluten-free as well, so gluten-free cookies became one of my specialties.

After five years of working at Roxy, I realized that although I loved action sports, it just wasn't my true passion. I really wanted to be spending my days baking. My boyfriend, Delaney, who came to Huntington Beach from Maui, was also ready for a change of scenery. This led us back to the quaint mountain town of Mammoth Lakes. Once we resettled there, it became clear that the town needed a place where locals could go to indulge in something sweet. It was the perfect time and place to open a bakery, the bakery that until now I had only dreamed about. My vision was to open a bakery that served nothing but cookies. Peanut butter cookies, chocolate chip cookies, coconut cookies, cookies with nuts, cookies without nuts, sweet and salty cookies, cookies with frosting, and many more. I shared my plan with a friend, not knowing that she and her husband would end up turning into my business partners.

Their involvement gave me the extra capital I needed to make it all happen. Soon thereafter, Dessert'D Organic Bake Shop was born, and Kimmy and Chris Benchetler have been part owners ever since. Six crazy weeks later, our doors were open and, true to my dream, we served nothing but cookies! (And milk, of course.) Slowly our menu expanded from soft and chewy cookies only to include French macarons. Then we added shortbreads and sandwich cookies. Not long after that came cookie pies and Florentines. Sure, we mixed in some cakes, pies, and ice cream, but our main focus is, and always will be, cookies. As our bake shop continued to grow we brought on another couple, Matt and Thea Zobel, as investors.

I think part of growing and evolving is sharing—sharing knowledge, lessons learned, and methods that work. Now that the bakery was doing so well, it made me think about what I should do next. And that's why I decided to write this book.

I want to share with you my tried and true cookie recipes. Some are from that little blue recipe box I've had with me since I was young. These are the ones I created for the people I love, like my dad, who inspired Dad's Coconut Chocolate Chip Cookies (page 21), the "cookie that started it all." It was the first cookie I learned to bake at high altitude. It was the cookie I baked for all my new friends in Mammoth when I moved away from home, the friends who became my family. It was the cookie I shared with Delaney and all my friends at Roxy. It was the cookie that, when my friends tasted it, they praised it and said I should open a bakery. And it's still one of my favorite cookies today.

In addition to sharing my favorite recipes, I am going to show you that baking gluten-free cookies is just as easy as baking regular cookies. Just because someone can't eat wheat doesn't mean they can't enjoy cookies. And you can give these cookies to anyone, because I promise you, they won't even know they are gluten-free! I'm also going to reveal that baking at high altitude is just as easy as baking at sea level or anywhere in between. Just because you live at eight thousand feet you don't have to put up with flat cookies. I'll show you that many cookie recipes can be made vegan. No need for dairy or eggs to make an indulgent and absolutely delicious cookie, just like my Sea Salt Dark Chocolate Chunk Cookies (page 50). It's all about having a recipe that works, and my recipes work.

I've organized the chapters to start with my easiest recipes first. As you hone your cookie-baking skills, you can move deeper into the book, and by the end you'll be ready for the more challenging recipes, like French macarons. The recipes within each chapter go from easiest to hardest as well.

Finally, like my mom, I believe in healthy eating, so I only use natural and organic ingredients. Pure, clean, and organic ingredients make up the best things—cookies included. I think everyone should be able to enjoy the simple pleasure of eating a well-baked cookie, one free of processed ingredients and artificial colors. I opened a bakery so people could get their cookie fix. And I want everyone to be able to enjoy them, whether they are gluten-free, they are vegan, they love chocolate, they hate chocolate, they're allergic to nuts, or they will eat a cookie only if it has frosting. Whatever kind of cookie you love, I've got you covered.

A WORD ABOUT ORGANICS

I hope you will use organic ingredients for all the recipes in this book, as I do at Dessert'D Organic Bake Shop and at home in my own kitchen. I believe that quality ingredients are just as important as a good recipe. Most people think of produce or dairy when they think of organic ingredients, and a lot of people don't see the need to make a cookie organic because it's already an indulgence. But I think that's exactly why you *should* bake with organic ingredients! If you're going to indulge, don't you want that treat to be made of the best possible ingredients? I certainly do.

Our customers really love the cookies we make, and for that I give a lot of the credit to the quality of ingredients I use. I always use organic flour, sugar, and flavorings, all made without synthetic pesticides, so that their flavors come through. Organic cane sugar is less processed than conventional granulated sugar, and it has a darker color that often provides a richer flavor, which in turn makes the cookie you're eating taste even better. Organic chocolate is also more flavorful than nonorganic versions, and it is free of the unnecessary additives usually added as preservatives.

When shopping for organic ingredients at the store, look for very short ingredients lists that don't include a lot of additives. For me, it is all about flavor—I want to eat the most chocolatey chocolate chip cookie, the sweetest buttercream-filled sandwich cookie, or a Lemon YiaYia Cookie that actually tastes like fresh lemon. And that's why I use organic ingredients. Throughout the book, I'll share some of my favorite brands, ones I use whenever I bake cookies. And I'll bet you'll be surprised to find that they aren't much more expensive than nonorganic ingredients. Remember, if you are going to treat yourself to cookies, make sure they are the best cookies ever!

BASIC INGREDIENTS

ONLY A FEW SIMPLE INGREDIENTS ARE NEEDED TO MAKE COOKIES. Keep your pantry and refrigerator stocked so you'll always be ready to whip up a batch.

Farm and Fridge

Most of these ingredients might already be in your fridge. Here I talk about my favorite kinds.

Butter

Butter is a key ingredient in cookies. I use butter in every single cookie (except for the vegan ones, of course!). At Dessert'D all our recipes are made with organic salted butter. My mom only had salted butter in our house when I was growing up, because she was a cook and not a baker. She hated unsalted butter, and now I know why—I mean, who wants to eat unsalted butter on their toast? When I started baking I used what we had at home, salted butter, and I've never changed that. If you prefer, you can use organic unsalted butter, but then you may want to add a little more salt to the recipes to get them to your liking. It's always best to get butter fresh from a farm if you can, but I know that is not always possible. I obsess over fresh butter when I can get it. The rest of the time I am forced to go to the market like everyone else. All butter can taste a little different, so find one you like and stick with it.

Eggs

The recipes in this book call for large organic eggs (with the exception of Crack Butter Cookies, page 116). If you can't find large eggs and only can get medium or extra-large, you can beat the eggs and then weigh them so you get the right amount. Too much egg can make your cookie dough very sticky and difficult to work with; too little can make it dry. One large egg weighs about 50 grams out of its shell. If you're using a different-size egg, just multiply how many eggs you need by 50 grams, and weigh your eggs after they are cracked and beaten, which will give you the correct amount of egg you need. You can always use any extra egg for breakfast the following morning.

Fruit

I love to use fresh fruits, preferably from a farmers' market, but I live in a town that is four square miles in size, and we rarely have them. If I leave town and go to the beach, I love going to the farmers' market there, and I'll load up on everything I can. But you can still get amazing fruit at your local grocery store if you know what you're looking for. The best thing is to use fruit that is in season. If you want to make Blueberry French Macarons (page 237) and it's not blueberry season, I suggest using frozen organic blueberries instead of buying subpar fresh ones. Fruit is frozen at its peak freshness, so don't be afraid of frozen fruit. Sometimes it's even better than what you can find fresh at the time. If you're making Strawberry Preserves (page 266), you can use frozen instead of fresh. But for the Lemon-Frosted Blueberry Cookies (page 34), it's better to use fresh because frozen berries have way more moisture in them. If you're going to use frozen berries for that recipe, thaw them in a mesh strainer overnight in the fridge—you'll see how much liquid comes out. Then you can use the thawed, drained berries in the cookies.

Milk and Cream

The recipes in this book that call for milk are meant to be made with organic whole milk. In a pinch you can substitute 2 percent, but never skim. You can also substitute unsweetened vanilla coconut milk for cow's milk in any recipe. Organic heavy whipping cream is another staple that we use a lot at Dessert'D. Our favorite brand is Organic Valley, but there are many others out there that are just as good.

Pantry

There are a few basic pantry staples I make sure to always have on hand.

Baking Powder and Baking Soda

Always check the dates on baking powder and baking soda. They quickly lose their strength after expiration. I prefer to buy aluminum-free versions; my favorites are from Frontier Co-Op.

Cocoa and Chocolate

My recipes use organic Dutch cocoa powder. I like the taste and richness of Dutch cocoa better than natural, which I feel is a little less sweet. If you prefer natural, you can use that instead. When choosing chocolate to bake with, it all comes down to taste. If you don't like the taste of the chocolate, you shouldn't bake with it. Choose organic milk chocolate, dark chocolate, and semisweet chocolate that you like to eat on its own. My favorites are SunSpire Organic Semi-Sweet Chocolate Chips, which you can find at your local market. And Mama Ganache is great for organic milk chocolate, dark chocolate, and white chocolate. Their dark chocolate is 70 percent, which I find strikes a nice balance between bitter and just sweet enough for cookies. Find them at www.mamaganache.com.

Corn Syrup

There is only one kind of organic corn syrup on the market these days, and it's made by Wholesome. This is the one you should get for all recipes. It is called Organic Light Corn Syrup. You'll need to have it on hand for making Florentines.

Flavors and Extracts

Flavors and extracts are different things, and though many people think they are interchangeable, they are not. A flavor is less concentrated than an extract. If you're going to substitute one for the other, make sure you're doing it correctly. For any of the recipes in this book, use this formula:

1 TEASPOON EXTRACT = 2 TEASPOONS FLAVOR

Flavors and extracts can also make or break your desserts as far as the flavor profile is concerned. Make sure you buy pure, organic flavors, and not ones that are labeled as syrups or imitation. There are lots of different brands out there for standard flavors like vanilla extract, almond flavor, or coconut extract. If you don't care for one, try another brand until you find one you like. Using good flavors and extracts can drastically alter the flavor of your cookies and take them from just okay to awesome. I love

Simply Organic vanilla extract, and it's really easy to find at your local market. Frontier Co-Op has the best organic lemon flavor, organic peppermint flavor, all-natural almond flavor, all-natural banana flavor, all-natural cherry flavor, all-natural coffee flavor, and more. The great thing about this company is that it is a co-op, so anyone can join. You can sign up on their website at www.frontiercoop.com, and you can also find this brand at a lot of health food stores.

Flour

ALL-PURPOSE FLOUR: This is an everyday flour and the one I call for most often in the book. Any organic brand should be sufficient, though I prefer unbleached if there is a choice. The grocery-store brand is fine—no need to worry about buying super-fancy flour. Save your money for ingredients that require spending a little more.

GLUTEN-FREE FLOUR: For the best results, use a gluten-free flour blend. Using only one type of flour, such as almond flour or coconut flour, will give you disappointing results. My favorite gluten-free flour blend is Namaste Organic Perfect Flour Blend. This is the brand we use at Dessert'D and the one I used to test all the recipes in this book. It's made up of organic sweet brown rice flour, organic brown rice flour, organic tapioca starch, organic arrowroot powder, and organic sorghum flour. I think it has wonderful flavor and texture. If you can't find it, look for mixes that use similar ingredients. King Arthur All-Purpose Gluten-Free Flour is also a good choice, though it's not organic. It has the added ingredient of potato starch. Cup4Cup is very much like King Arthur and is my third choice. Many flour blends also include xanthan gum, which is needed to bind baked goods together when there is no gluten.

OTHER FLOURS: A few recipes call for organic coconut flour or organic almond flour. When that's the case, don't substitute. These flours have gotten much easier to find at most grocery stores. Almond flour is used in all the French macaron recipes, so it is a must for your pantry. There are also a few recipes that call for cake flour. There is not an organic cake flour on the market yet, so my top choice is King Arthur Unbleached Cake Flour.

Food Coloring

I usually prefer my foods without added colors. I do admit, though, that sometimes desserts are a little prettier with a pastel hue, especially French macarons. The desserts in this book were all tested with the dyes we use at Dessert'D, from ColorKitchen. They are powdered dyes made from vegetables, and you can use them to get amazing pastel or bright colors. I love that these dyes are powders, because you're not adding any liquid to the recipes. The pastel colors are really easy to make because they require just a small amount of powder, but if you want a brighter hue you can simply double the amount of color used. Find these dyes on their website, www.colorkitchenfoods.com. I recommend using only ColorKitchen for dying French macarons. But if you're just dyeing frostings, then you can use India Tree Nature's Colors liquid dyes: www.indiatree.com.

Honey

I always like to buy organic, raw, local honey because it potentially offers more antioxidants and greater anti-inflammatory benefits than more processed honey, which is pasteurized and thus has a longer shelf life but at the cost of those health advantages. It just doesn't make sense to me to eat something that has had its health benefits removed. Local honey may be able to help build your immune system, which is great for those who suffer from allergies, so why not buy it if you can?

Molasses

The organic molasses I recommend is made by Wholesome, and it's what we use at Dessert'D. This is actually blackstrap molasses, even though the label doesn't say it. So, when you're shopping and wondering if you're purchasing the right one, if it's from Wholesome, then you are! Molasses is made during the production of sugar, and molasses has a higher sugar content than blackstrap molasses. I use blackstrap molasses along with sugar in all my recipes, hence why I use blackstrap molasses.

Peanut Butter

Organic peanut butter. Yes, that is the kind that has a good amount of oil on top and is usually separated when you buy it. I like to buy peanut butter that contains only two ingredients: organic dry roasted peanuts and sea salt. I know it can be a pain—trust me, we go through ridiculous amounts of these jars at the bakery, and we have to stir up every single one! But the quality and taste of that peanut butter blow the doors off any other kind. Here's a trick to make it a bit easier to work with. Dump an entire jar of peanut butter into your stand mixer bowl fitted with the paddle attachment, and mix on low until creamy. Then put it right back in the jar.

Salt

Salt is used in sweet baking because it brings out the flavors of all the other ingredients without making everything salty. I like to use fine sea salt for all my recipes. I avoid iodized salt because it doesn't actually bring out flavors very well.

Spices

Spices are an amazing way to add more flavor to your cookies. I use organic ground spices in all the recipes in this book, which can be found at any local market. Two of my favorite brands are Simply Organic and Frontier Co-Op. Spices last for about six months for best flavor, so buy small amounts if it's something you don't use all the time. You can get both of these brands at Frontier Co-Op: www.frontiercoop.com.

Sprinkles

Everyone loves sprinkles, I won't deny it. But what I don't love is the artificial colors and weird stuff they put in sprinkles. That's why I use all-natural sprinkles made with dyes from vegetables. At Dessert'D we use a few different brands. Our pastel rainbow sprinkles are from India Tree, and they are called Nature's Colors Carnival Mix. They are dyed with things like turmeric, annatto, and beet juice. They are a little lighter in color than traditional rainbow sprinkles, but I really like the pastel look. We also use India Tree's Natural Chocolate Sprinkles. These are delicious because they actually taste like chocolate, unlike other sprinkles. You can find them on their website, www.indiatree.com. If you want traditional bright rainbow sprinkles, pick up Rainbow Sprinkles from ColorKitchen. Their colors are brighter, and they are made with almost the exact same ingredients as the ones from India Tree. Find them at

www.colorkitchenfoods.com. A brand called Ticings produces all-natural sprinkles from real chocolate. They also make colored sprinkles from white chocolate and natural vegetable dyes. These are the best-tasting sprinkles out there for sure. The only drawback with Ticings sprinkles is that they don't react very well in the oven, so don't use them in recipes like Sprinkled Shortbread (page 109). They are better for decorating the tops of cookies and biscotti after they come out of the oven. You can find them on their website, www.ticings.com.

Sugar

CANE SUGAR: All the recipes in this book are intended to be made with organic cane sugar, which is easy to find, even at chain grocery stores. Organic sugar looks quite different than regular sugar—it is usually a little darker and more tan in color because it's less processed (and more flavorful!) than white sugar, and the crystals are usually larger. If you don't use organic sugar, your baked goods will probably come out lighter in color.

POWDERED SUGAR: This is also known as confectioners' sugar. All the recipes here call for powdered sugar to be sifted because it can sometimes clump, especially if it's been sitting in the pantry for a little while. Sifting will help avoid lumps in your cookies or frostings.

BROWN SUGAR: I use organic dark brown sugar for all recipes. You may choose to use organic light brown sugar, though it won't have as much flavor and your finished product won't be as dark in color. Wholesome is my favorite brand if you're going to buy it. But you can actually make your own Brown Sugar (page 246), which is super easy—and you can get the exact shade of darkness you're looking for. It also lasts longer than store bought.

Vanilla Bean

I like to use organic ground vanilla bean in place of vanilla extract for many recipes. Vanilla bean has a different flavor than vanilla extract. It is earthier and richer, whereas extract is a little sweeter. I really like the pairing of vanilla bean with chocolate, which is why I use it in a lot of chocolate cookies, like the Double Chocolate Chip Cookies (page 22). And with the Vanilla Bean Florentines (page 176), using vanilla bean instead of vanilla extract gives the cookie more balance because Florentines are already very sweet. If you don't have organic ground vanilla bean, you can substitute vanilla extract. Use this formula:

½ TEASPOON GROUND VANILLA BEAN = 1 TEASPOON VANILLA EXTRACT

ESSENTIAL TOOLS

THERE ARE A FEW PIECES OF BAKING EQUIPMENT I RECOMMEND YOU HAVE.

Candy Molds

You will need ½-ounce candy molds to make the Caramel Candies (page 250).

Cookie Cutter

You will need a 2½-inch circle cookie cutter to make the Nostalgic Sandwich Cookies (page 162). If you don't have a cookie cutter, a round glass with the same diameter will work in a pinch.

Cookie Scoops

To make perfectly sized mini cookies like the Coconut Minis (page 49) and the Chocolate Chip Minis (page 105), I use a 1.3-ounce cookie scoop (you can find one on Amazon), which gives them their unique shape and texture. It's essential to have this tool for these cookies as it makes them the correct size, shape, and width in proportion to the baking time.

Cookie Sheets

Most recipes in the book call for two 18 x 13-inch cookie sheets (also known as half sheet pans), but in some cases you might need four. This is the size I use all the time. I use aluminum cookie sheets, and that's what I recommend for you, too. A different (darker) finish on the cookie sheets might yield different results in the oven.

Digital Food Scale

I highly recommend that you buy a kitchen scale, because I believe that a failure to measure properly is the main reason why many recipes don't turn out successfully. At Dessert'D, we measure everything by weight—everything! I can't stress enough how much more accurate it is. If you are measuring by weight, your ingredients will be measured accurately every single time. And that allows you to focus on honing your skills. Scales come in many sizes and prices, so there is sure to be the perfect one out there for you. Make sure the scale can measure in both ounces and grams.

Digital Thermometer

I prefer to use a digital thermometer for everything from Tempered Chocolate (page 268) to heating the batter for Florentines to the perfect temperature. I use the thermometer because I like to be precise to get the best results—that's kinda the point, right?

Food Processor

It is necessary to have a food processor to make every single Florentine in this book. And Florentines are probably going to be some of your new favorite cookies, so buy one if you don't already have one. You can also use it to make almond flour if it's hard for you to find at the grocery store, and you'll need almond flour to make French macarons. A few other recipes call for a food processor as well, to use for steps ranging from grinding the nuts for Snickerdoodle Pecan Biscotti (page 84) to processing graham crackers for S'more Sandwich Cookies (page 157).

Ice Cream Maker

Two of my favorite noncookie recipes and my personal must-haves for enjoying cookies are Chocolate Fro-Yo (page 254) and Coconut Ice Cream (page 261). You will need an ice cream maker, or you can use the ice cream maker attachment for the KitchenAid Stand Mixer, like I do. It works great!

Measuring Cups

Whenever measuring liquids, I always recommend using measuring cups instead of a liquid measuring cup. Measuring cups are always more accurate because you can measure exactly to the brim. With a liquid measuring cup, if you aren't looking at it straight on, your measurement could be off. And with a cookie like a Florentine you want to be as precise as possible.

Measuring Spoons

Make sure you have a good set of measuring spoons. You should be measuring to the brim of the spoon.

Mixing Bowls

You should have a couple of good mixing bowls. You'll need a heatproof mixing bowl for tempering chocolate. And although I don't recommend plastic for most things, it is best to use a plastic mixing bowl for making Florentines because the batter is hot, and a metal or glass bowl might become too hot to touch.

Parchment Paper

Almost all the recipes in this book call for lining the cookie sheets with parchment paper. This will help immensely when removing the cookies after baking, not to mention making it easier to clean up! My favorite parchment paper is EcoCraft Bake 'N' Reuse Pan Liners. They are brown, not white, and you can reuse the precut sheets many times. This really helps when you are making a lot of cookies (like I do).

Piping Bag and Tips

A piping bag and decorating tips will come in very handy for filling sandwich cookies and Florentines. And when making French macarons, using a piping bag is actually a necessity to get that beautiful, perfectly round shape. I highly recommend buying 16-inch to 18-inch reusable piping bags, which can be washed and reused multiple times. I've often seen them sold in packs of three. When you cut the end off the pastry bag, make sure you're not cutting it larger than the decorating tip you will put inside. In a pinch you can use a zip-top plastic bag, though those don't work well if you need to use a decorating tip.

For decorating tips, I use the Ateco brand. Ateco decorating tips will correspond with the numbers I provide throughout the book.

To fill the piping bag with batter or frosting, have ready a tall glass or a small vase, put the bag in it, and fold the edges over the sides. This leaves you with both hands free to easily fill your piping bag. Pour in the batter or frosting, and you're ready to go. At the bakery, we use stainless-steel milkshake cups for this step, and they work perfectly!

Pot

For the recipes in this book, a 2-quart pot is the only size you will need. I prefer stainless steel, especially since I sometimes call to whisk ingredients together, such as for Chocolate Fro-Yo (page 254) and Chocolate Milk (page 258), and if you use a nonstick pot you could scratch it. You will also use the pot as part of a double boiler to melt or temper chocolate for dipping cookies.

Sharp Knife

Make sure you have a chef's knife that has been well sharpened. When cutting biscotti, for example, you want the cuts to be clean so each cookie is sliced evenly and looks beautiful.

Sifter

Powdered sugar and cocoa powder should always be sifted before using to remove clumps. Make sure to get a fine-mesh sifter that can hold 3 to 4 cups.

Spatulas

You'll need a regular rubber spatula (for filling sandwich cookies with frosting, for example). But you should have a high-temperature silicone spatula as well, one that can withstand up to 500°F. Use the high-heat spatula when you make things like Caramel Sauce (page 253) and Florentines so you don't melt or ruin your other spatulas.

Stand Mixer with Paddle & Whisk Attachments

It is not necessary to have a stand mixer to make all the recipes in this book, but some do require it. Many of these recipes make a stiff dough that would take a lot of arm strength to mix by hand. If you are making macarons or frosting, you will thank me for telling you to use a stand mixer, believe me. Each chapter includes Tips and Tricks that will tell you which recipes truly require a stand mixer.

Timer

The difference between well-baked and burnt can be incredibly small. Always use a timer, whether it's the one on your oven or a separate one. Although it's true that after making literally thousands of cookies, I have a sort of internal clock that "knows" when they are done, that skill is a long time coming. When it comes to baking cookies, you don't want to be disappointed because you left them in the oven 1 or 2 minutes longer than is ideal. For perfect cookies every time, use a timer.

SOFT AND CHEWY COOKIES

THE FIRST SOFT AND CHEWY COOKIE I EVER MADE WAS chocolate chip, using the recipe off the back of a bag of Nestlé chocolate chips. My mom has never been into baking, like I am. When I was young and asked her if I could bake something, she'd pull out a box or a bag from the pantry and tell me to "follow the recipe on the back." We didn't have many family recipes that were desserts, aside from YiaYia Cookies (page 124), so that's how I learned to bake. Betty Crocker, Nestlé, and Duncan Hines, thank you!

After I mastered that chocolate chip recipe, I got bored baking and eating the same cookie. This was before everyone had smartphones and could Google or Pinterest another recipe in no time. I still had dial-up internet when I was learning to bake. So I started experimenting on my own. One day, I was in the kitchen messing around with chocolate chip cookie dough, and my dad asked me to add coconut to the dough because he used to swoon over a coconut chocolate chip cookie from his childhood. To please him I added the coconut, and that was the very first time I made Dad's Coconut Chocolate Chip Cookies (page 21).

After that, I had a hard time making basic chocolate chip cookies, because they were so much better with coconut. That inspired me to step out of the box and try even more flavors. Dad's Coconut Chocolate Chip Cookies were the inspiration, and they turned into the base recipe for all the other cookies in this chapter.

Tips and Tricks

Mixing

Although I call for a stand mixer in this chapter, you can make all the recipes here with a bowl and a wooden spoon or a rubber spatula. The mixer is easier and faster, but either method will do. Don't make the mistake of using a hand mixer; it can whip the butter too much, adding air to the cookies, which you don't want to do.

Butter

All the recipes in this chapter use butter softened to room temperature. If you are planning to bake cookies, depending on the weather and the temperature of your kitchen, leave the butter out on the counter for at least 2 hours or even overnight, and it will be the ideal consistency. Butter can be softened in the microwave, but be careful to heat it in 10-second intervals to avoid melting it. Melted butter will not combine with the sugar in the same way as softened butter and will change the results of your cookies. Perfectly soft butter should leave an indentation if you press your finger into it gently.

Eggs

You'll notice that all the recipes in this chapter say to mix the eggs "slightly." Since you will be rolling these cookies into balls with your hands, you don't want the dough to be too sticky. It should be workable to the touch and easily molded with your hands. I have found that if the eggs are overmixed, the dough is stickier. If you do happen to overmix, and you find your cookie dough very sticky, just pop the bowl of cookie dough in the fridge for 10 minutes or so until it's easier to work with.

Gluten-Free Cookies

When you're rolling balls of gluten-free cookie dough, make them a tad larger than the recipe notes. Gluten-free flour doesn't cause the dough to rise as high, so it won't spread as much as the dough of non-gluten-free cookies because of the difference in properties between gluten-free and all-purpose flour. For example, if the recipe says to make the cookie into a 2¼-inch disk, make a 2½-inch disk if using gluten-free flour.

Storing

To ensure that your cookies stay soft and chewy, store them in an airtight container at room temperature so they don't dry out. If you live in a very humid climate, they'll be fine out on the counter or in a cookie jar for a couple of days. Use an airtight container with a lid, a zip-top plastic bag, or wrap them tightly in plastic wrap. All the cookies in this chapter will stay fresh for up to one week when stored properly.

This is the cookie that started it all...my love of cookies, my love of baking, and my dream to open a bake shop. And it is still one of my all-time favorites. I like to eat these cookies when they have just cooled so they aren't hot but the chocolate chips are still melty.

Makes 24

½ cup (113 grams) salted butter, softened

¼ cup plus 2 tablespoons (85 grams) cane sugar

¼ cup plus 2 tablespoons (85 grams) packed dark brown sugar

1 teaspoon vanilla extract

2 large eggs

1⅔ cups plus 2 tablespoons (227 grams) all-purpose flour

½ teaspoon baking soda

½ teaspoon fine sea salt

¾ cup (142 grams) semisweet chocolate chips

1⅓ cups (85 grams) unsweetened wide-flake coconut

Preheat the oven to 375°F. Line 2 cookie sheets with parchment paper.

In the bowl of a stand mixer fitted with the paddle attachment, add the butter, cane sugar, dark brown sugar, and vanilla extract. Mix on low until combined and there are no chunks of butter.

Add the eggs and mix slightly, enough to break the yolks.

In a separate bowl, whisk together the flour, baking soda, and sea salt.

Add the flour mixture to the butter mixture, and mix on low until it is almost combined; you should still see streaks of flour. Add the chocolate chips and coconut, and mix until a stiff dough forms.

Using your hands, form the dough into 24 balls and place them on the prepared cookie sheets, leaving 1 inch between them (12 should fit on each cookie sheet). Flatten each ball slightly. They should look like disks that are about 2¼ inches in diameter.

Bake for 11 minutes, or until the cookies are lightly browned on the edges and bottom. Let cool completely on the cookie sheets.

Store in an airtight container at room temperature for up to 7 days.

>>> GLUTEN-FREE—REPLACE THE ALL-PURPOSE FLOUR WITH 1½ CUPS PLUS 1 TABLESPOON (240 GRAMS) GLUTEN-FREE FLOUR BLEND.

>>> HIGH ALTITUDE—BAKE AT 375°F FOR 8 MINUTES, OR UNTIL THE COOKIES ARE LIGHTLY BROWNED ON THE EDGES AND BOTTOM.

DOUBLE CHOCOLATE CHIP COOKIES

I never had a soft and chewy chocolate cookie until I created one for myself. Like many people, I love chocolate more than anything, so it's odd to me that you don't see more chocolate cookies out in the world. My husband calls these "brownie cookies" because they are so soft, gooey, and chocolatey, like a really good brownie. For the ultimate chocolate lover, I recommend sandwiching a couple of these around some homemade Chocolate Fro-Yo (page 254).

Makes 24

½ cup (113 grams) salted butter, softened

½ cup (113 grams) cane sugar, plus more for dusting

½ cup (113 grams) packed dark brown sugar

2 large eggs

1½ cups plus 1 tablespoon (198 grams) all-purpose flour

½ cup (43 grams) Dutch cocoa powder, sifted

½ teaspoon ground vanilla bean

1½ teaspoons baking powder

½ teaspoon fine sea salt

¾ cup (142 grams) semisweet chocolate chips

Preheat the oven to 375°F. Line 2 cookie sheets with parchment paper.

In the bowl of a stand mixer fitted with the paddle attachment, add the butter, cane sugar, and dark brown sugar. Mix on low until combined and there are no chunks of butter.

Add the eggs and mix slightly, enough to break the yolks.

In a separate bowl, whisk together the flour, cocoa powder, vanilla bean, baking powder, and sea salt.

Add the flour mixture to the butter mixture, and mix on low until it is almost combined; you should still see streaks of flour. Add the chocolate chips, and mix until a stiff dough forms.

Using your hands, form the dough into 24 balls and place them on the prepared cookie sheets, leaving 1 inch between them (12 should fit on each cookie sheet). Flatten each ball slightly. They should look like disks that are about 2¼ inches in diameter.

Bake for 11 minutes, or until the cookies are set and cracked on top. Sprinkle the cookies with cane sugar immediately after they come out of the oven. Let cool completely on the cookie sheets.

Store in an airtight container at room temperature for up to 7 days.

>>> GLUTEN-FREE—REPLACE THE ALL-PURPOSE FLOUR WITH 1⅓ CUPS (212 GRAMS) GLUTEN-FREE FLOUR BLEND.

>>> HIGH ALTITUDE—BAKE AT 375°F FOR 8 MINUTES, OR UNTIL THE COOKIES LOOK SET AND CRACKED ON TOP.

This is not your grandma's oatmeal cookie—I have added a few extra special ingredients to make it even better. But it's a very flexible recipe. Don't like walnuts? Use peanuts or almonds instead. But make sure you use the Sun Drops, because they are the best part! Sun Drops (SunSpire brand) are small candy-coated chocolates made with all-natural ingredients, including the colorings. You could also use Unreal Milk Chocolate Gems.

Makes 24

$\frac{1}{2}$ cup (113 grams) salted butter, softened

$\frac{1}{4}$ cup plus 2 tablespoons (85 grams) cane sugar

$\frac{1}{4}$ cup plus 2 tablespoons (85 grams) packed dark brown sugar

1 teaspoon vanilla extract

2 large eggs

$1\frac{1}{3}$ cups (170 grams) all-purpose flour

2 teaspoons cinnamon

$\frac{1}{2}$ teaspoon baking soda

$\frac{1}{2}$ teaspoon fine sea salt

1 cup plus 2 tablespoons (113 grams) rolled oats

Heaping $\frac{1}{2}$ cup (113 grams) Sun Drops

Heaping $\frac{1}{2}$ cup (70 grams) chopped walnuts

Scant $\frac{1}{2}$ cup (70 grams) raisins

Scant $\frac{1}{2}$ cup (85 grams) peanut butter chips

Preheat the oven to 375°F. Line 2 cookie sheets with parchment paper.

In the bowl of a stand mixer fitted with the paddle attachment, add the butter, cane sugar, dark brown sugar, and vanilla extract. Mix on low until combined and there are no chunks of butter.

Add the eggs and mix slightly, enough to break the yolks.

In a separate bowl, whisk together the flour, cinnamon, baking soda, and sea salt. Add the flour mixture to the butter mixture, and mix on low until almost combined. Add the oats, Sun Drops, walnuts, raisins, and peanut butter chips, and mix on low until a stiff dough forms.

Using your hands, form the dough into 24 balls, and place them on the prepared cookie sheets, leaving 1 inch between them (12 should fit on each cookie sheet). Flatten each ball slightly. They should look like disks that are about 2¼ inches in diameter.

Bake for 11 minutes, or until the edges look dry and the tops look cracked; the center should still look a little gooey. Let cool completely on the cookie sheets.

Store in an airtight container at room temperature for up to 7 days.

>>> GLUTEN-FREE—USE GLUTEN-FREE OATS. REPLACE THE ALL-PURPOSE FLOUR WITH 1 CUP PLUS 3 TABLESPOONS (185 GRAMS) GLUTEN-FREE FLOUR BLEND.

>>> HIGH ALTITUDE—BAKE AT 375°F FOR 8 MINUTES, OR UNTIL THE EDGES LOOK DRY AND THE TOPS LOOK CRACKED; THE CENTER SHOULD STILL LOOK A LITTLE GOOEY.

This cookie is from the early days, before the bake shop opened. It's one of those recipes that came together perfectly, and it hasn't changed a bit since I first created it. Customers come back for this one again and again.

Makes 24

DOUGH

1/2 cup (113 grams) salted butter, softened

1/2 cup (113 grams) cane sugar

1/2 cup (113 grams) packed dark brown sugar

1 teaspoon vanilla extract

3/4 cup plus 1 tablespoon (227 grams) peanut butter

1 large egg

1 large egg yolk

1 cup plus 2 tablespoons (142 grams) all-purpose flour

1/2 teaspoon fine sea salt

1/2 teaspoon baking soda

3/4 cup (142 grams) semisweet chocolate chips

1/2 cup (43 grams) chopped pretzels

TOPPING

1 teaspoon cane sugar

1 teaspoon fine sea salt

Preheat the oven to 375°F. Line 2 cookie sheets with parchment paper.

To make the dough: In the bowl of a stand mixer fitted with the paddle attachment, add the butter, cane sugar, dark brown sugar, and vanilla extract. Mix on low until combined and there are no chunks of butter.

Add the peanut butter, egg, and egg yolk, and mix slightly (2 to 3 rotations on the stand mixer or a couple of folds with a spatula). Do not overmix.

In a separate bowl, whisk together the flour, sea salt, and baking soda.

Add the flour mixture to the butter mixture, and mix on low until almost combined. You still want to see a little bit of flour. Add the chocolate chips and pretzels, and mix until thoroughly combined.

Using your hands, form the dough into 24 balls and place them on the prepared cookie sheets, leaving 1 inch between them (12 should fit on each cookie sheet). Flatten each ball slightly. They should look like disks that are about 2 inches in diameter.

Bake for 11 minutes, or until the tops look cracked and set.

To make the topping: In a small dish, mix together the cane sugar and sea salt.

Sprinkle the cookies with some of the topping immediately after they come out of the oven. Let cool completely on the cookie sheets.

Store in an airtight container at room temperature for up to 7 days.

>>> GLUTEN-FREE—USE GLUTEN-FREE PRETZELS. REPLACE THE ALL-PURPOSE FLOUR WITH 1 CUP (155 GRAMS) GLUTEN-FREE FLOUR BLEND.

>>> HIGH ALTITUDE—BAKE AT 375°F FOR 8 MINUTES, OR UNTIL THE COOKIES LOOK CRACKED AND SET.

I have always loved the taste of honey in baked goods like graham crackers, cereal, and bread. As a child deprived of sweets, I think I realized that honey was my ticket to finding sweetness in other ways besides candy and desserts, and it became my sneaky way of getting a sugar fix. These cookies taste of sweet honey and almonds, and the white chocolate drizzle on top makes them just sweet enough.

Makes 20

½ cup (113 grams) salted butter, softened

½ cup (113 grams) cane sugar

2 tablespoons packed dark brown sugar

2 tablespoons raw honey

1 teaspoon vanilla extract

2 large eggs

2¼ cups plus 1 tablespoon (298 grams) all-purpose flour

½ teaspoon cinnamon

½ teaspoon baking soda

½ teaspoon fine sea salt

1 cup (113 grams) sliced raw almonds with their skins

½ cup (85 grams) chopped white chocolate

Preheat the oven to 375°F. Line 2 cookie sheets with parchment paper.

In the bowl of a stand mixer fitted with the paddle attachment, add the butter, cane sugar, dark brown sugar, honey, and vanilla extract. Mix on low until combined and there are no chunks of butter.

Add the eggs and mix slightly, enough to break the yolks.

In a separate bowl, whisk together the flour, cinnamon, baking soda, and sea salt. Add the flour mixture to the butter mixture, add the almonds, and mix on low until a stiff dough forms.

Using your hands, form the dough into 20 balls and place them on the prepared cookie sheets, leaving 1 inch between them (10 should fit on each cookie sheet). Flatten each ball slightly. They should look like disks that are about 2¼ inches in diameter.

Bake for 11 minutes, or until the cookies are puffed and lightly browned. Let cool completely on the cookie sheets.

Temper the white chocolate using the technique on page 268.

Using a spoon, drizzle the white chocolate over the tops of the cookies. Place the cookies in the fridge, and allow to set for about 1 hour before serving.

Store in an airtight container at room temperature for up to 7 days.

>>> GLUTEN-FREE—REPLACE THE ALL-PURPOSE FLOUR WITH 2 CUPS (310 GRAMS) GLUTEN-FREE FLOUR BLEND.

>>> HIGH ALTITUDE—BAKE AT 375°F FOR 8 MINUTES, OR UNTIL THE COOKIES ARE PUFFED AND LIGHTLY BROWNED.

DOUGH

1/2 cup (113 grams) salted butter, softened

1/2 cup (113 grams) cane sugar

1/2 cup (71 grams) powdered sugar, sifted

1 teaspoon vanilla extract

2 large eggs

2 1/4 cups plus 1 tablespoon (298 grams) all-purpose flour

1/4 teaspoon cinnamon

1 1/2 teaspoons baking powder

1/2 teaspoon fine sea salt

GLAZE

2 cups plus 3 tablespoons (311 grams) powdered sugar, sifted

1/3 cup (30 grams) Dutch cocoa powder, sifted

1/4 teaspoon almond flavor

1/4 cup milk

All-natural rainbow sprinkles

On the best Saturdays of my childhood, my dad and I would walk our golden retriever, Brighty, to Java, the neighborhood café. They served coffee and the best chocolate-glazed cake donuts in the entire city of Chicago. If you didn't get there early enough, the donuts would be sold out. I could hardly wait the eight blocks it took to walk home before tearing open the paper bag and eating one. This recipe was created in honor of those days and those donuts. I know it will be difficult, but the best way to enjoy these cookies is to make them 24 hours before you plan to eat them, because the glaze is best (and most donut-like) when it's allowed to set for a day. If you live in a dry and/or high-altitude climate, wrap the entire cookie sheet with plastic wrap—the most important thing is to make sure it's airtight—so they won't dry out while the glaze is setting.

Makes 24

Preheat the oven to 375°F. Line 2 cookie sheets with parchment paper.

To make the dough: In the bowl of a stand mixer fitted with the paddle attachment, add the butter, cane sugar, powdered sugar, and vanilla extract. Mix on low until combined and there are no chunks of butter.

Add the eggs and mix slightly, enough to break the yolks.

In a separate bowl, whisk together the flour, cinnamon, baking powder, and sea salt. Add the flour mixture to the butter mixture, and mix on low until a stiff dough forms.

Using your hands, form the dough into 24 balls and place them on the prepared cookie sheets, leaving 1 inch between

them (12 should fit on each cookie sheet). Flatten each ball slightly. They should look like disks that are about 2 inches in diameter.

Bake for 11 minutes, or until the cookies are cracked on top and set. Let cool completely on the cookie sheets.

To make the glaze: In a medium bowl, whisk together the powdered sugar, cocoa powder, almond flavor, and milk until you have a smooth glaze.

Using a butter knife or small spatula, spread the glaze on each cookie, and top with rainbow sprinkles. Cover the cookies and let the glaze set for at least 24 hours before serving or stacking the cookies.

Store in an airtight container at room temperature for up to 7 days.

>>> GLUTEN-FREE—REPLACE THE ALL-PURPOSE FLOUR WITH 2 CUPS (310 GRAMS) GLUTEN-FREE FLOUR BLEND.

>>> HIGH ALTITUDE—BAKE AT 375°F FOR 8 MINUTES, OR UNTIL THE COOKIES ARE CRACKED ON TOP AND SET.

One of my favorite things about Christmas is gingerbread. And gingerbread cookies definitely come first on my list. After growing up in a household that was usually free of sweets, it always surprised me that my mom would stock the pantry with gingerbread men around the holidays. If she hadn't stopped me, I would probably have eaten all of them. And when I realized you could put icing on them, I knew I had found the ultimate Christmas cookie of my dreams.

Makes 24

1/2 cup (113 grams) salted butter, softened

1/2 cup (113 grams) cane sugar

1/2 cup (113 grams) packed dark brown sugar

1/4 cup (85 grams) Wholesome Molasses

1 teaspoon vanilla extract

2 large eggs

2 1/2 cups plus 3 tablespoons (340 grams) all-purpose flour

1 teaspoon cinnamon

1 teaspoon ginger

1 teaspoon cloves

1/2 teaspoon baking soda

1/2 teaspoon fine sea salt

Cookie Glaze (page 262)

Preheat the oven to 375°F. Line 2 cookie sheets with parchment paper.

In the bowl of a stand mixer fitted with the paddle attachment, add the butter, cane sugar, dark brown sugar, molasses, and vanilla extract. Mix on low until combined and there are no chunks of butter.

Add the eggs and mix slightly, enough to break the yolks.

In a separate bowl, whisk together the flour, cinnamon, ginger, cloves, baking soda, and sea salt. Add the flour mixture to the butter mixture, and mix on low until a stiff dough forms.

Using your hands, form the dough into 24 balls and place them on the prepared cookie sheets, leaving 1 inch between them (12 should fit on each cookie sheet). Flatten each ball slightly. They should look like disks that are about 2 1/4 inches in diameter.

Bake for 11 minutes, or until the cookies look puffed and cracked on top. Let cool completely on the cookie sheets.

Using a butter knife or a small spatula, spread the cookie glaze on top of each cookie. Cover the cookies and let the glaze set for at least 24 hours before serving or stacking the cookies.

Store in an airtight container at room temperature for up to 7 days.

>>> GLUTEN-FREE—REPLACE THE ALL-PURPOSE FLOUR WITH 2 1/4 CUPS PLUS 1 TEASPOON (354 GRAMS) GLUTEN-FREE FLOUR BLEND.

>>> HIGH ALTITUDE—BAKE AT 375°F FOR 8 MINUTES, OR UNTIL THE COOKIES LOOK PUFFED AND CRACKED ON TOP.

This is one of the original recipes I created for Dessert'D. Every time I bake these cookies I have sweet memories of summer, no sleep, endless cookie baking, and pure hustling as I worked to make the bakery successful.

Makes 24

½ cup (113 grams) salted butter, softened

½ cup (113 grams) cane sugar

½ cup (71 grams) powdered sugar, sifted

1 teaspoon vanilla extract

2 large eggs

2¼ cups plus 1 tablespoon (298 grams) all-purpose flour

½ teaspoon cinnamon

1½ teaspoons baking powder

½ teaspoon fine sea salt

6 ounces (170 grams) fresh blueberries

Cookie Glaze, made with the lemon variation (page 262)

Preheat the oven to 375°F. Line 2 cookie sheets with parchment paper.

In the bowl of a stand mixer fitted with the paddle attachment, add the butter, cane sugar, powdered sugar, and vanilla extract. Mix on low until combined and there are no chunks of butter.

Add the eggs and mix slightly, enough to break the yolks.

In a separate bowl, whisk together the flour, cinnamon, baking powder, and sea salt. Add the flour mixture to the butter mixture, and mix on low until a stiff dough forms. Using a wooden spoon or a rubber spatula, gently fold in the blueberries, being careful not to break too many.

Using your hands, form the dough into 24 balls and place them on the prepared cookie sheets, leaving 1 inch between them (12 should fit on each cookie sheet). Flatten each ball slightly. They should look like disks that are about 2 inches in diameter.

Bake for 11 minutes, or until the edges of the cookies and the areas around the blueberries look dry. Let cool completely on the cookie sheets.

Using a butter knife or a small spatula, spread lemon cookie glaze on top of each cookie. Cover the cookies and let the glaze set for at least 24 hours before serving or stacking the cookies.

Store in an airtight container at room temperature for up to 7 days.

>>> GLUTEN-FREE—REPLACE THE ALL-PURPOSE FLOUR WITH 2 CUPS (310 GRAMS) GLUTEN-FREE FLOUR BLEND.

>>> HIGH ALTITUDE—BAKE AT 375°F FOR 8 MINUTES, OR UNTIL THE EDGES OF THE COOKIES AND THE AREAS AROUND THE BLUEBERRIES LOOK DRY.

Once you realize how easy it is to make brown butter, you will bake this recipe over and over again. It has a nutty, slightly sweet flavor that adds a subtle but craveable quality to this cookie.

Makes 18

Heaping $1/3$ cup (85 grams) Brown Butter (page 245), at room temperature

$1/2$ cup (113 grams) packed dark brown sugar

$1/4$ cup (57 grams) cane sugar, plus more for topping

1 teaspoon vanilla extract

2 large eggs

$1^2/3$ cups (212 grams) all-purpose flour

$1/2$ teaspoon baking soda

$1/2$ teaspoon fine sea salt

$3/4$ cup (106 grams) chopped milk chocolate

Preheat the oven to 375°F. Line 2 baking sheets with parchment paper.

In the bowl of a stand mixer fitted with the paddle attachment, add the brown butter, dark brown sugar, cane sugar, and vanilla extract, and mix on low until combined.

Add the eggs and mix slightly, enough to break the yolks.

In a separate bowl, whisk together the flour, baking soda, and sea salt. Add the flour mixture to the butter mixture, and mix on low until combined. Add the chopped milk chocolate, and mix on low to combine.

Using your hands, form the dough into 18 balls and place them on the prepared cookie sheets, leaving 1 inch between them (9 should fit on each cookie sheet). Flatten each ball slightly. They should look like disks that are about $2\frac{1}{4}$ inches in diameter.

Bake for 11 minutes, or until the cookies are lightly puffed and set.

Sprinkle the cookies with cane sugar immediately after they come out of the oven. Let cool completely on the cookie sheets.

Store in an airtight container at room temperature for up to 7 days.

>>> GLUTEN-FREE—REPLACE THE ALL-PURPOSE FLOUR WITH A SCANT 1$1/2$ CUPS (226 GRAMS) GLUTEN-FREE FLOUR BLEND.

>>> HIGH ALTITUDE—BAKE AT 375°F FOR 8 MINUTES, OR UNTIL THE COOKIES ARE LIGHTLY PUFFED AND SET.

When I first created these cookies at the bake shop, we filled them with Caramel Sauce (page 253) and rolled out tiny dough tops to cover them before baking. Once we started making them by the hundreds, that got old really fast. After a quick redevelopment of the recipe, we decided to tuck Caramel Candies (page 250) inside the dough. So much faster and easier. Sometimes you can create something better than you thought possible.

Makes 24

DOUGH

1/2 cup (113 grams) salted butter, softened

1/4 cup plus 2 tablespoons (85 grams) cane sugar

1/4 cup plus 2 tablespoons (85 grams) packed dark brown sugar

1 teaspoon vanilla extract

2 large eggs

2 cups (255 grams) all-purpose flour

1/2 teaspoon baking soda

1/2 teaspoon fine sea salt

3/4 cup (142 grams) semisweet chocolate chips

12 Caramel Candies, each cut in half (page 250)

TOPPING

1 teaspoon cane sugar

1 teaspoon fine sea salt

Preheat the oven to 375°F. Line 2 cookie sheets with parchment paper.

To make the dough: In the bowl of a stand mixer fitted with the paddle attachment, add the butter, cane sugar, dark brown sugar, and vanilla extract. Mix on low until combined and there are no chunks of butter.

Add the eggs and mix slightly, enough to break the yolks.

In a separate bowl, whisk together the flour, baking soda, and sea salt. Add the flour mixture to the butter mixture, and mix on low until a stiff dough forms. Add the chocolate chips, and mix until combined.

Using your hands, form the dough into 24 balls and place them on the prepared cookie sheets, leaving 1 inch between them (12 should fit on each cookie sheet). Place 1 caramel half on top of each ball, and press it down into the center. Fold the dough over the caramel so it's completely covered. Flatten each ball slightly. They should look like disks that are 2 inches in diameter.

Bake for 11 minutes, or until lightly browned.

To make the topping: In a small dish, mix together the cane sugar and sea salt.

Sprinkle the cookies with the topping immediately after they come out of the oven. Let cool completely on the cookie sheets.

Store in an airtight container at room temperature for up to 7 days.

>>> GLUTEN-FREE—REPLACE THE ALL-PURPOSE FLOUR WITH 1$^3/_4$ CUPS (269 GRAMS) GLUTEN-FREE FLOUR BLEND.

>>> HIGH ALTITUDE—BAKE AT 375°F FOR 8 MINUTES, OR UNTIL LIGHTLY BROWNED.

These are the perfect cookies to bring to Thanksgiving. They smell like fall and they are way more interesting than another apple pie. This recipe uses Caramel Candies (page 250), so be sure to make those ahead of time.

Makes 24

$1/2$ cup (113 grams) salted butter, softened

$1/4$ cup plus 2 tablespoons (85 grams) cane sugar

$1/4$ cup plus 2 tablespoons (85 grams) packed dark brown sugar

1 teaspoon vanilla extract

2 large eggs

2 cups (255 grams) all-purpose flour

2 teaspoons cinnamon

$1/2$ teaspoon baking soda

$1/2$ teaspoon fine sea salt

1 medium apple (about $4^1/2$ ounces/120 grams), Fuji, Gala, or Cripps Pink, chopped into $1/2$-inch cubes

12 Caramel Candies (page 250), each cut in half

Preheat the oven to 375°F. Line 2 cookie sheets with parchment paper.

In the bowl of a stand mixer fitted with the paddle attachment, add the butter, cane sugar, dark brown sugar, and vanilla extract. Mix on low until all the ingredients are combined and there are no chunks of butter.

Add the eggs and mix just enough to break the yolks.

In a separate bowl, whisk together the flour, cinnamon, baking soda, and sea salt. Add the flour mixture to the butter mixture, and mix on low until a stiff dough forms. Add the chopped apple, and mix until evenly combined.

Using your hands, form the cookie dough into 24 balls and place them on the prepared cookie sheets, leaving 1 inch between them (12 should fit on each cookie sheet).

Place 1 caramel half on top of each ball, and press it down into the center. Fold the dough over the caramel so it's completely covered. Flatten each ball slightly. They should look like disks that are 2 inches in diameter.

Bake for 11 minutes, or until lightly browned. Let cool completely on the cookie sheets.

Store in an airtight container at room temperature for up to 7 days.

>>> GLUTEN-FREE—REPLACE THE ALL-PURPOSE FLOUR WITH $1^3/4$ CUPS (269 GRAMS) GLUTEN-FREE FLOUR BLEND.

>>> HIGH ALTITUDE—BAKE AT 375°F FOR 8 MINUTES, OR UNTIL LIGHTLY BROWNED.

My first word was "woof," and ever since, I have been obsessed with dogs. When I was one year old, my dad took me to pick out my first dog, a golden retriever we named Brighton. He was my best friend—we were inseparable. I dressed him up in jewelry and hats. We went biking, sledding, and Rollerblading together. We even ate cookies together. By that, I mean I ate his dog biscuits with him. Yeah, they weren't good, but we were bonding. When Brighton passed away, I thought I'd never have a best friend like him again. Years went by, and then I got Otto—three-quarters pug and one-quarter basset hound—and we've been BFFs for over a dozen years. Otto had some allergies when he was a puppy, and we found out that he was slightly allergic to chicken. Many dog treats include chicken by-products, so I created my own. Otto loves them! He knows what the bag looks like when I bring them home from the bake shop, and he gets just as excited as I do when I eat cookies. Like mother, like pugger, I guess.

Makes 36

1 cup plus 2 tablespoons (142 grams) all-purpose flour

$^3/_4$ cup (71 grams) rolled oats

$^1/_2$ teaspoon baking soda

$^3/_4$ cup plus 1 tablespoon (227 grams) peanut butter

$^1/_4$ cup plus 3 tablespoons (142 grams) raw honey

2 large eggs

Preheat the oven to 375°F. Line 2 cookie sheets with parchment paper.

In the bowl of a stand mixer fitted with the paddle attachment, add the flour, oats, and baking soda, and mix together on low for 2 to 3 turns.

Add the peanut butter, honey, and eggs, and mix on low until a stiff dough forms.

Using your hands, form the dough into 36 balls and place them on the prepared cookie sheets, leaving 1 inch between them (18 should fit on each cookie sheet). Flatten each ball slightly. They should look like disks that are about 1½ inches in diameter.

Bake for 9 to 10 minutes, or until the edges are slightly brown. Let cool completely on the cookie sheets.

Store in an airtight container at room temperature for up to 2 weeks.

>>> GLUTEN-FREE—REPLACE THE ALL-PURPOSE FLOUR WITH 1 CUP (155 GRAMS) GLUTEN-FREE FLOUR BLEND.

>>> HIGH ALTITUDE—BAKE AT 375°F FOR 8 MINUTES, OR UNTIL THE EDGES ARE SLIGHTLY BROWN.

VEGAN COOKIES

"WHAT IS A VEGAN COOKIE?!"

I'm from the Midwest, the land of meat and potatoes, so that was my reaction when Kimmy, my friend and partner at Dessert'D, asked me to bake vegan cookies before we opened our bake shop.

I knew that vegans eat no animal products—that means no meat, dairy, cheese, or eggs. Many don't eat honey either. For my vegan recipes I had to figure out a way to replace the butter, eggs, and milk. I never shy away from a challenge, and I knew that if I created delicious vegan cookies they would be popular with both vegans and customers with a dairy intolerance. So I started test baking batches of vegan cookies. I tried all kinds of ingredients to replace the butter, eggs, and milk, and trust me, they were not all good (at least I didn't think so). I experimented with applesauce, different oils, almond butter, and peanut butter. But with peanut butter or almond butter I was limited to having nuts in all the cookies, which would make them off-limits to those with nut allergies. Kimmy kept taking home all my test batches, and I couldn't believe she was eating them willingly because I was spitting them out! My goal was to create a vegan cookie that was a delicious cookie first, one you didn't have to preface with, "Oh well, it's good for a vegan cookie."

I finally found the best butter substitute: coconut! I love coconut. It's sweet, it's fatty like butter, it's good for you, and it's actually tasty. Because of its sweetness, I felt it would be okay in lots of different vegan cookies, no matter the flavor, and I was right. Now I use Earth Balance Coconut Spread in all my vegan cookies. It is a blend of a couple of different oils, including coconut oil. The taste is pretty neutral—not overwhelmingly coconut flavored—which makes it the perfect vegan substitute for butter.

To replace the eggs, I landed on simply adding a nondairy milk. I didn't want to use a nut milk, which would not work for those with nut allergies, so I ended up using coconut milk. My favorite is So Delicious Unsweetened Vanilla Coconut Milk. And that substitute worked perfectly. You can replace the coconut milk with any other dairy-free milk you like, but coconut milk has the most neutral flavor, and it also has a smooth consistency, which is important.

The last step was figuring out what kind of chocolate to put in them. Because, let's be real, you can't have a cookie unless it can be made with chocolate chips. Semi-sweet chocolate chips are made with milk, so they aren't vegan. No milk chocolate, no semisweet chocolate—that left dark chocolate. But be careful when buying dark chocolate, because some lesser-quality brands contain milk or milk by-products. You have to read the ingredients. The dark chocolate I use at Dessert'D comes from Mama Ganache: www.mamaganache.com. It comes in little disks, which I chop into all sorts of sizes.

Now you know all my secrets! My vegan cookies don't have to be labeled "vegan." They are simply delicious cookies in their own right.

Tips and Tricks

Coconut Spread

Earth Balance Coconut Spread is made of organic coconut oil, organic canola oil, organic palm oil, and organic extra-virgin coconut oil. It comes in a small tub. You can find it in the refrigerator section at most health food stores and in some chain grocery stores. You can switch out coconut spread with other vegan butter options if you like; I just don't think they taste as good. My second choice is Earth Balance Vegan Buttery Sticks, which will work for all the recipes in this chapter. But don't use straight oil or the cookies will have a different texture. Coconut spread should be used at room temperature—soft, but not melted (which will change the consistency of the final baked cookie, and not in a good way). If you leave it out on the counter for at least 20 minutes before using it, you should be good to go.

Mixing

The key to making excellent vegan cookies is mixing the coconut spread and the sugars together thoroughly. This step is the same as it is for regular cookies, where you cream the butter with the sugar completely. Use a stand mixer set on low to medium speed, and mix until the blend is smooth and lacks any visible white chunks.

Baking

A telltale sign of doneness for cookies is how brown they get. It's a little harder to tell when vegan cookies are done because butter is what promotes browning, and coconut spread does not brown in the same way. Instead, look at the centers of the cookies. They should be set and not doughy. And don't worry—your vegan cookies will get some color in the oven, just not as much as cookies made with butter.

Storing

All of these cookies will last for up to seven days when stored in an airtight container at room temperature. If you're making crunchy cookies, like the Coconut Minis (page 49) or PB&J Thumbprints (page 68), you can leave them out on the counter or store them in a cookie jar. But if you live in a humid climate, then they, too, should be stored in an airtight container so they keep their crisp texture.

One of my favorite things is coconut. And I don't know why, but if you miniaturize anything, it just makes it better (I can prove it by how many of these cookies I sell). These are the perfect snack for any time of day.

Makes 40 to 45

1/2 cup (113 grams) cane sugar

1/4 cup plus 2 tablespoons (85 grams) coconut oil

2 tablespoons packed dark brown sugar

2 teaspoons coconut extract

1 teaspoon vanilla extract

1/2 cup (113 grams) coconut spread

2 cups (255 grams) all-purpose flour

2/3 cup (57 grams) unsweetened finely shredded coconut

1/2 teaspoon fine sea salt

Preheat the oven to 350°F. Line 2 cookie sheets with parchment paper.

In the bowl of a stand mixer fitted with the paddle attachment, add the cane sugar, coconut oil, dark brown sugar, coconut extract, and vanilla extract. Mix on low until combined and there are no chunks of coconut oil.

Add the coconut spread, and mix until combined and there are no chunks of coconut spread.

Add the flour, finely shredded coconut, and sea salt, and mix on low until a stiff dough forms.

Using a 1.3-ounce cookie scoop, scoop dough onto the prepared cookie sheets (20 to 23 should fit on each cookie sheet). Space them about 1 inch apart. Flatten each one slightly.

Bake for 16 minutes, or until the cookies are lightly browned. Let cool completely on the cookie sheets.

Store in an airtight container at room temperature for up to 7 days.

>>> GLUTEN-FREE—REPLACE THE ALL-PURPOSE FLOUR WITH A SCANT 1/2 CUP (43 GRAMS) COCONUT FLOUR AND 1 1/4 CUPS (198 GRAMS) GLUTEN-FREE FLOUR BLEND.

>>> HIGH ALTITUDE—BAKE AT 350°F FOR 15 MINUTES, OR UNTIL THE COOKIES ARE LIGHTLY BROWNED.

SEA SALT DARK CHOCOLATE CHUNK COOKIES

This is one of our best-selling cookies at Dessert'D, period. And it's vegan! This is what I mean when I say that first I want a cookie to taste amazing. If it's vegan or gluten-free, I just call that a bonus.

Makes 20

DOUGH

1/2 cup (113 grams) coconut spread

1/4 cup plus 2 tablespoons (85 grams) cane sugar

1/4 cup plus 2 tablespoons (85 grams) packed dark brown sugar

1 1/4 teaspoons vanilla extract

2 1/4 cups plus 3 tablespoons (312 grams) all-purpose flour

1/2 teaspoon baking soda

1/2 teaspoon fine sea salt

1/2 cup (118 milliliters) unsweetened vanilla coconut milk

1 cup (142 grams) chopped dark chocolate

TOPPING

1 teaspoon cane sugar

1 teaspoon fine sea salt

Preheat the oven to 375°F. Line 2 cookie sheets with parchment paper.

To make the dough: In the bowl of a stand mixer fitted with the paddle attachment, add the coconut spread, cane sugar, dark brown sugar, and vanilla extract. Mix on low until combined and there are no chunks of coconut spread.

In a separate bowl, whisk together the flour, baking soda, and sea salt.

Add the coconut milk and the flour mixture to the sugar mixture, and mix on low until almost completely combined. Add the chopped dark chocolate, and mix until a stiff dough forms.

Using your hands, form the dough into 20 balls and place them on the prepared cookie sheets, leaving 1 inch between them (10 should fit on each cookie sheet). Flatten each ball slightly. They should look like disks that are about 2½ inches in diameter.

Bake for 11 minutes, or until the edges are lightly browned.

To make the topping: In a small dish, mix together the cane sugar and sea salt.

Sprinkle the cookies with the topping immediately after they come out of the oven. Let cool completely on the cookie sheets.

Store in an airtight container at room temperature for up to 7 days.

>>> GLUTEN-FREE—REPLACE THE ALL-PURPOSE FLOUR WITH 2 CUPS (310 GRAMS) GLUTEN-FREE FLOUR BLEND.

>>> HIGH ALTITUDE—BAKE AT 375°F FOR 8 MINUTES, OR UNTIL THE EDGES ARE LIGHTLY BROWNED.

Cool mint and dark chocolate have always been friends. These soft sugar cookies remind me of Peppermint Patties. And they're even better if you sandwich Coconut Ice Cream (page 261) between them.

Makes 20

½ cup (113 grams) coconut spread

½ cup (113 grams) cane sugar, plus more for topping

½ cup (71 grams) powdered sugar, sifted

1¼ teaspoons peppermint flavor

1 teaspoon vanilla extract

2¾ cups plus 2 teaspoons (354 grams) all-purpose flour

1½ teaspoons baking powder

½ teaspoon fine sea salt

½ cup (118 milliliters) unsweetened vanilla coconut milk

1 cup (142 grams) chopped dark chocolate

Preheat the oven to 375°F. Line 2 cookie sheets with parchment paper.

In the bowl of a stand mixer fitted with the paddle attachment, add the coconut spread, cane sugar, powdered sugar, peppermint flavor, and vanilla extract. Mix on low until combined and there are no chunks of coconut spread.

In a separate bowl, whisk together the flour, baking powder, and sea salt.

Add the coconut milk and the flour mixture to the sugar mixture, and mix on low until almost completely combined. Add the chopped dark chocolate, and mix until a stiff dough forms.

Using your hands, form the dough into 20 balls and place them on the prepared cookie sheets, leaving 1 inch between them (10 should fit on each cookie sheet). Flatten each ball slightly. They should look like disks that are about 2¾ inches in diameter.

Bake for 11 minutes, or until the cookies are set and cracked on top. Sprinkle the cookies with cane sugar immediately after they come out of the oven. Let cool completely on the cookie sheets.

Store in an airtight container at room temperature for up to 7 days.

>>> GLUTEN-FREE—REPLACE THE ALL-PURPOSE FLOUR WITH 2¼ CUPS PLUS 1 TEASPOON (354 GRAMS) GLUTEN-FREE FLOUR BLEND.

>>> HIGH ALTITUDE—BAKE AT 375°F FOR 8 MINUTES, OR UNTIL THE COOKIES ARE SET AND CRACKED ON TOP.

CHOCOLATE PECAN PRETZEL COOKIES

This cookie is the perfect combination of all the holiday snacking I like to do over Christmas break. Chocolate, nuts, and salty pretzels—what more could anyone want?

Makes 16

DOUGH

½ cup (113 grams) packed dark brown sugar

¼ cup plus 2 tablespoons plus 2 teaspoons (91 grams) coconut spread

2 tablespoons cane sugar

1¼ cups plus 3 tablespoons (184 grams) all-purpose flour

½ cup (43 grams) Dutch cocoa powder

½ teaspoon ground vanilla bean

1½ teaspoons baking powder

½ teaspoon fine sea salt

½ cup (118 milliliters) unsweetened vanilla coconut milk

½ cup (43 grams) chopped pretzels

Scant ½ cup (57 grams) chopped pecans

TOPPING

1 teaspoon cane sugar

1 teaspoon fine sea salt

Preheat the oven to 375°F. Line 2 cookie sheets with parchment paper.

To make the dough: In the bowl of a stand mixer fitted with the paddle attachment, add the dark brown sugar, coconut spread, and cane sugar. Mix on low until combined and there are no chunks of coconut spread.

In a separate bowl, whisk together the flour, cocoa powder, vanilla bean, baking powder, and sea salt.

Add the coconut milk and the flour mixture to the sugar mixture, and mix on low until a stiff dough forms. Add the chopped pretzels and pecans, and mix on low until combined.

Using your hands, form the dough into 16 balls and place them on the prepared cookie sheets, leaving 1 inch between them (8 should fit on each cookie sheet). Flatten each ball slightly. They should look like disks that are about 2½ inches in diameter.

Bake for 11 minutes, or until the cookies are slightly puffed and dry.

To make the topping: In a small bowl, mix together the cane sugar and sea salt.

Sprinkle the cookies with some of the topping immediately after they come out of the oven. Let cool completely on the cookie sheets.

Store in an airtight container at room temperature for up to 7 days.

>>> GLUTEN-FREE—USE GLUTEN-FREE PRETZELS. REPLACE THE ALL-PURPOSE FLOUR WITH 1 CUP PLUS 3 TABLESPOONS (184 GRAMS) GLUTEN-FREE FLOUR BLEND.

>>> HIGH ALTITUDE—BAKE AT 375°F FOR 8 MINUTES, OR UNTIL THE COOKIES ARE SLIGHTLY PUFFED AND DRY.

I love to name things "kitchen sink" because it's an invitation to literally add anything you want. This version is my absolute favorite, but you could replace the dried blueberries with dried cranberries, replace the almonds with walnuts or pecans, or even omit the chocolate. This cookie is a great blank canvas for creating your own flavor combinations.

Makes 20

½ cup (113 grams) coconut spread

¼ cup plus 2 tablespoons (85 grams) cane sugar

¼ cup plus 2 tablespoons (85 grams) packed dark brown sugar

1 teaspoon vanilla extract

2¼ cups plus 3 tablespoons (312 grams) all-purpose flour

½ teaspoon baking soda

½ teaspoon fine sea salt

½ cup (118 milliliters) unsweetened vanilla coconut milk

½ cup plus 2 tablespoons (85 grams) chopped dark chocolate

½ cup (85 grams) dried blueberries

½ cup (57 grams) sliced almonds with their skins

⅔ cup (57 grams) unsweetened finely shredded coconut

Preheat the oven to 375°F. Line 2 cookie sheets with parchment paper.

In the bowl of a stand mixer fitted with the paddle attachment, add the coconut spread, cane sugar, dark brown sugar, and vanilla extract. Mix on low until combined and there are no chunks of coconut spread.

In a separate bowl, whisk together the flour, baking soda, and sea salt.

Add the coconut milk and flour mixture to the sugar mixture, and mix on low until a stiff dough forms. Add the dark chocolate, blueberries, and almonds, and mix on low until combined.

Place the shredded coconut in a small bowl. Set aside.

Using your hands, form the dough into 20 balls and place them on the prepared cookie sheets, leaving 1 inch between them (10 should fit on each cookie sheet). Flatten each ball slightly. They should look like disks that are about 2½ inches in diameter.

Dip the top of each cookie into the shredded coconut, and return it to the cookie sheet.

Bake for 11 minutes, or until the coconut is toasted. Let cool completely on the cookie sheets.

Store in an airtight container at room temperature for up to 7 days.

>>> GLUTEN-FREE—REPLACE THE FLOUR WITH 2 CUPS (312 GRAMS) GLUTEN-FREE FLOUR BLEND.

>>> HIGH ALTITUDE—BAKE AT 375°F FOR 8 MINUTES, OR UNTIL THE COCONUT IS TOASTED.

Although I wasn't introduced to snickerdoodles until I was an adult, I like to think I'm making up for lost time. I'm always looking for new ways to make them more fun. Adding brown sugar gives these classics even more flavor and dimension.

Makes 20

DOUGH

1/2 cup (113 grams) coconut spread

1/4 cup plus 2 tablespoons (85 grams) cane sugar

1/4 cup plus 2 tablespoons (85 grams) packed dark brown sugar

1 teaspoon vanilla extract

2 1/4 cups plus 3 tablespoons (312 grams) all-purpose flour

3/4 teaspoon cinnamon

1/2 teaspoon baking soda

1/2 teaspoon fine sea salt

1/2 cup (118 milliliters) unsweetened vanilla coconut milk

TOPPING

2 tablespoons cane sugar

1 teaspoon cinnamon

Preheat the oven to 375°F. Line 2 cookie sheets with parchment paper.

To make the dough: In the bowl of a stand mixer fitted with the paddle attachment, add the coconut spread, cane sugar, dark brown sugar, and vanilla extract. Mix on low until combined and there are no chunks of coconut spread.

In a separate bowl, whisk together the flour, cinnamon, baking soda, and sea salt.

Add the coconut milk and the flour mixture to the sugar mixture, and mix on low until a stiff dough forms.

To make the topping: Combine the cane sugar and cinnamon in a small bowl. Set aside.

Using your hands, form the dough into 20 balls and place them on the prepared cookie sheets, leaving 1 inch between them (10 should fit on each cookie sheet). Flatten each ball slightly. They should look like disks that are about 2¼ inches in diameter.

Dip the top of each ball of dough into the cinnamon and sugar mixture, and return it to the cookie sheet.

Bake for 11 minutes, or until they are light brown and a little cracked on top. Let cool completely on the cookie sheets.

Store in an airtight container at room temperature for up to 7 days.

>>> GLUTEN-FREE—REPLACE THE ALL-PURPOSE FLOUR WITH 2 CUPS (312 GRAMS) GLUTEN-FREE FLOUR BLEND.

>>> HIGH ALTITUDE—BAKE AT 375°F FOR 8 MINUTES, OR UNTIL THEY ARE LIGHT BROWN AND A LITTLE CRACKED ON TOP.

GINGER SNAPS

I love ginger snaps. I make them all year round because when I close my eyes and eat them it feels like Christmas. And that is one of my favorite times of the year.

Makes 20

DOUGH

¹/₂ cup (113 grams) coconut spread

¹/₂ cup (113 grams) cane sugar

¹/₂ cup (113 grams) packed dark brown sugar

¹/₄ cup (85 grams) Wholesome Molasses

1 teaspoon vanilla extract

2 ³/₄ cups plus 2 teaspoons (354 grams) all-purpose flour

1 teaspoon cinnamon

1 teaspoon ginger

1 teaspoon cloves

¹/₂ teaspoon baking soda

¹/₂ teaspoon fine sea salt

¹/₄ cup plus 1 tablespoon (73 milliliters) unsweetened vanilla coconut milk

TOPPING

2 tablespoons cane sugar

1 teaspoon cinnamon

Preheat the oven to 375°F. Line 2 cookie sheets with parchment paper.

To make the dough: In the bowl of a stand mixer fitted with the paddle attachment, add the coconut spread, cane sugar, dark brown sugar, molasses, and vanilla extract. Mix on low until combined and there are no chunks of coconut spread.

In a separate bowl, whisk together the flour, cinnamon, ginger, cloves, baking soda, and sea salt.

Add the coconut milk and flour mixture to the sugar mixture, and mix on low until a stiff dough forms.

To make the topping: Combine the cane sugar and cinnamon in a small bowl. Set aside.

Using your hands, form the dough into 20 balls and place them on the prepared cookie sheets, leaving 1 inch between them (10 should fit on each cookie sheet). Flatten each ball slightly. They should look like disks that are about 2¼ inches in diameter.

Dip the top of each ball of dough into the cinnamon and sugar mixture, and return it to the cookie sheet.

Bake for 11 minutes, or until they are golden-brown and cracked on top. Let cool completely on the cookie sheets.

Store in an airtight container at room temperature for up to 7 days.

>>> GLUTEN-FREE—REPLACE THE FLOUR WITH 2¹/₄ CUPS PLUS 1 TEASPOON (354 GRAMS) GLUTEN-FREE FLOUR BLEND.

>>> HIGH ALTITUDE—BAKE AT 375°F FOR 8 MINUTES, OR UNTIL THEY ARE GOLDEN-BROWN AND CRACKED ON TOP.

Soft and chewy sugar cookies with lemon zest. These are made with organic lemon flavor, but you could use extract if you wanted to. Just remember to use half as much extract as you would flavor, because it's more concentrated.

Makes 20

½ cup (113 grams) coconut spread

½ cup (113 grams) cane sugar, plus ¼ cup (57 grams) for rolling

½ cup (71 grams) powdered sugar, sifted

2 tablespoons lemon flavor

2 cups (255 grams) all-purpose flour

1½ teaspoons baking powder

½ teaspoon fine sea salt

⅓ cup (78 milliliters) unsweetened vanilla coconut milk

Zest from 1 lemon

Preheat the oven to 375°F. Line 2 cookie sheets with parchment paper.

In the bowl of a stand mixer fitted with the paddle attachment, add the coconut spread, cane sugar, powdered sugar, and lemon flavor. Mix on low until combined and there are no chunks of coconut spread.

In a separate bowl, whisk together the flour, baking powder, and sea salt.

Add the coconut milk, flour mixture, and lemon zest to the sugar mixture, and mix on low until a stiff dough forms.

Place the sugar for rolling in a small dish, and set aside.

Using your hands, form the dough into 20 balls, and roll each one in sugar. Place the dough balls on the prepared cookie sheets, leaving 1 inch between them (10 should fit on each cookie sheet).

Bake for 11 minutes, or until the cookies are set and cracked on top. Let cool completely on the cookie sheets.

Store in an airtight container at room temperature for up to 7 days.

>>> GLUTEN-FREE—REPLACE THE ALL-PURPOSE FLOUR WITH 1⅔ CUPS (255 GRAMS) GLUTEN-FREE FLOUR BLEND.

>>> HIGH ALTITUDE—BAKE AT 375°F FOR 8 MINUTES, OR UNTIL THE COOKIES ARE SET AND CRACKED ON TOP.

Oatmeal cookies were something I lived for as a child—weird, right? That's not usually a kid's favorite cookie, but because I rarely got sweet things, they were pretty special to me, and they still are today. These Oatmeal Drop Cookies include some of my favorite ingredients: cinnamon, coconut, and Cookie Glaze (page 262).

Makes 26

¼ cup plus 3 tablespoons (105 grams) coconut spread

¼ cup plus 1 tablespoon (68 grams) cane sugar

¼ cup plus 1 tablespoon (68 grams) packed dark brown sugar

1 teaspoon vanilla extract

1 cup (127 grams) all-purpose flour

1 teaspoon cinnamon

½ teaspoon baking soda

½ teaspoon fine sea salt

1 cup (100 grams) rolled oats

¼ cup plus 2 tablespoons (89 milliliters) unsweetened vanilla coconut milk

½ cup (57 grams) sliced almonds with their skins

Cookie Glaze, made with the vegan coconut variation (page 262)

Preheat the oven to 375°F. Line 2 cookie sheets with parchment paper.

In the bowl of a stand mixer fitted with the paddle attachment, add the coconut spread, cane sugar, dark brown sugar, and vanilla extract. Mix on low until combined and there are no chunks of coconut spread.

In a separate bowl, whisk together the flour, cinnamon, baking soda, sea salt, and oats.

Add the coconut milk and the flour mixture to the sugar mixture, and mix on low until almost combined. Add the almonds, and mix on low until a stiff dough forms.

Using a 1.3-ounce cookie scoop or a spoon, drop about 1 tablespoon of dough onto the cookie sheet. Continue with the rest of the dough, making sure to leave 1 inch between cookies (13 should fit on each cookie sheet).

Bake for 11 minutes, or until the edges are dry and the tops are cracked. The center will still look a little gooey. Let cool completely on the cookie sheets.

Using a spoon, drizzle cookie glaze over the top of each cookie.

Store in an airtight container at room temperature for up to 7 days.

>>> GLUTEN-FREE—USE GLUTEN-FREE OATS. REPLACE THE ALL-PURPOSE FLOUR WITH ¾ CUP PLUS 1 TABLESPOON (127 GRAMS) GLUTEN-FREE FLOUR BLEND.

>>> HIGH ALTITUDE—BAKE AT 375°F FOR 8 MINUTES, OR UNTIL THE EDGES ARE DRY AND THE TOPS ARE CRACKED. THE CENTER WILL STILL LOOK A LITTLE GOOEY.

I created these cookies to make up for all the beautiful, big sugar cookies I longed for and was never allowed to buy when I went to the market with my mom as a girl. I'll always remember how amazing they looked, with their colorful sprinkles—and I never got to have even one. But I can now. And so can you.

Makes 20

¹/₂ cup plus 2 tablespoons (142 grams) cane sugar

¹/₂ cup (113 grams) coconut spread

¹/₂ cup (71 grams) powdered sugar, sifted

2 cups (255 grams) all-purpose flour

¹/₂ teaspoon ground vanilla bean

1¹/₂ teaspoons baking powder

¹/₂ teaspoon fine sea salt

¹/₄ teaspoon cinnamon

¹/₃ cup (78 milliliters) unsweetened vanilla coconut milk

Cookie Glaze, made with the vegan variation (page 262)

Rainbow sprinkles, for topping

Preheat the oven to 375°F. Line 2 cookie sheets with parchment paper.

In the bowl of a stand mixer fitted with the paddle attachment, add the cane sugar, coconut spread, and powdered sugar. Mix on low until combined and there are no chunks of coconut spread.

In a separate bowl, whisk together the flour, vanilla bean, baking powder, sea salt, and cinnamon.

Add the coconut milk and the flour mixture to the sugar mixture, and mix on low until a stiff dough forms.

Using your hands, form the dough into 20 balls and place them on the prepared cookie sheets, leaving 1 inch between them (10 should fit on each cookie sheet). Flatten each ball slightly. They should look like disks that are about 2 inches in diameter.

Bake for 11 minutes, or until they are set and cracked on top. Let cool completely on the cookie sheets.

Using a butter knife or small spatula, spread cookie glaze on top of each cookie. Sprinkle rainbow sprinkles on top. Cover the cookies and let the glaze set for at least 24 hours before serving or stacking the cookies.

Store in an airtight container at room temperature for up to 7 days.

>>> GLUTEN-FREE—REPLACE THE ALL-PURPOSE FLOUR WITH 1²/₃ CUPS (255 GRAMS) GLUTEN-FREE FLOUR BLEND.

>>> HIGH ALTITUDE—BAKE AT 375°F FOR 8 MINUTES, OR UNTIL THEY ARE SET AND CRACKED ON TOP.

I hated the combination of peanut butter and jelly when I was a kid. I ate only plain peanut butter sandwiches, and I just didn't understand why anyone liked jam, jelly, or preserves. Now I can't believe I missed out on so many years of the perfect flavor pairing. I make up for it by eating these cookies, a lot.

Makes 24

1/4 cup plus 2 tablespoons (85 grams) coconut spread

1/4 cup plus 2 tablespoons (85 grams) cane sugar

1/4 cup plus 2 tablespoons (85 grams) packed dark brown sugar

1 teaspoon vanilla extract

1 1/3 cups (170 grams) all-purpose flour

1/2 teaspoon fine sea salt

1/2 cup plus 2 1/2 tablespoons (177 grams) peanut butter

Strawberry Preserves (page 266)

Preheat the oven to 350°F. Line 2 cookie sheets with parchment paper.

In the bowl of a stand mixer fitted with the paddle attachment, add the coconut spread, cane sugar, dark brown sugar, and vanilla extract. Mix on low until combined and there are no chunks of coconut spread.

In a separate bowl, whisk together the flour and sea salt.

Add the peanut butter and the flour mixture to the sugar mixture, and mix on low until a stiff dough forms.

Using your hands, form the dough into 24 balls and place them on the prepared cookie sheets, leaving 1 inch between them (12 should fit on each cookie sheet).

Press your thumb into each ball of dough to create an indentation. Fill the hole with strawberry preserves. Place the cookie sheets in the refrigerator for 10 minutes.

Transfer the cookie sheets to the oven and bake for 11 minutes, or until the cookies are set and lightly browned on the bottom. Let cool completely on the cookie sheets.

Store in an airtight container at room temperature for up to 7 days.

>>> GLUTEN-FREE—REPLACE THE ALL-PURPOSE FLOUR WITH A SCANT 1/2 CUP (43 GRAMS) COCONUT FLOUR AND 1 CUP (155 GRAMS) GLUTEN-FREE FLOUR BLEND.

>>> HIGH ALTITUDE—BAKE AT 350°F FOR 8 MINUTES, OR UNTIL THE COOKIES ARE SET AND LIGHTLY BROWNED ON THE BOTTOM.

~~~~~~

Cookie pies are my version of a sandwich cookie, but the cookies are soft and chewy instead of crispy. I felt they needed their own name, because not all sandwich cookies are created equal.

Makes 12 sandwiches

DOUGH

$1/2$ cup (113 grams) coconut spread

$1/2$ cup (113 grams) cane sugar, plus more for topping

$1/2$ cup (113 grams) packed dark brown sugar

1 teaspoon vanilla extract

$1\frac{1}{4}$ cups plus 2 tablespoons (177 grams) all-purpose flour

$1/2$ teaspoon baking soda

$1/2$ teaspoon fine sea salt

$3/4$ cup plus 1 tablespoon (227 grams) peanut butter

$2\frac{1}{2}$ tablespoons unsweetened vanilla coconut milk

FILLING

1 cup plus 3 tablespoons (170 grams) powdered sugar, sifted

2 tablespoons unsweetened vanilla coconut milk

$1/2$ teaspoon banana flavor

TOPPING

1 cup (142 grams) chopped dark chocolate

Preheat the oven to 375°F. Line 2 cookie sheets with parchment paper.

To make the dough: In the bowl of a stand mixer fitted with the paddle attachment, add the coconut spread, cane sugar, dark brown sugar, and vanilla extract. Mix on low until combined and there are no chunks of coconut spread.

In a separate bowl, whisk together the flour, baking soda, and sea salt.

Add the peanut butter, coconut milk, and flour mixture to the sugar mixture, and mix on low until a stiff dough forms.

Using your hands, form the dough into 24 balls and place them on the prepared cookie sheets, leaving 1 inch between them (12 should fit on each cookie sheet). Flatten each ball slightly. They should look like disks that are about 2¼ inches in diameter.

Bake for 11 minutes, or until the tops are cracked and set. Sprinkle the cookies with cane sugar immediately after they come out of the oven. Let cool completely on the cookie sheets.

To make the filling: In a medium bowl whisk together the powdered sugar, coconut milk, and banana flavor until smooth.

Turn over 12 of the cookies, spread each one with some of the filling, top each with another cookie, and return the sandwiches to the cookie sheets. Place the cookie sheets in the freezer for at least 15 minutes. This will set the filling and keep the cookie sandwiches from sliding apart when dipping.

For the topping: Temper the dark chocolate using the technique on page 268.

Remove the cookies from the freezer. Dip half of each cookie into the melted chocolate, and return it to the cookie sheet. Place the cookie sheets in the refrigerator for at least 1 hour to set the chocolate.

Store in an airtight container at room temperature for up to 7 days (or in the refrigerator if you live in a really warm climate).

>>> GLUTEN-FREE—REPLACE THE ALL-PURPOSE FLOUR WITH 1 CUP PLUS 2 TABLESPOONS (177 GRAMS) GLUTEN-FREE FLOUR BLEND.

>>> HIGH ALTITUDE—BAKE AT 375°F FOR 8 MINUTES, OR UNTIL THE TOPS ARE CRACKED AND SET.

BISCOTTI

LONG, SKINNY, AND INCREDIBLY CRUNCHY, biscotti originated in Italy. Their name means "twice baked." And that's literally how you make them. The dough is mixed, baked, cut into pieces, and then baked again, which is why they are so crispy. They are ideal for dipping in hot drinks like coffee or tea, but, really, anytime is a good time to eat them.

Biscotti is actually the plural form of the word *biscotto.* But no one ever makes just one! Because biscotti are so dry, they last longer than other cookies, and they are perfect for wrapping up and giving as a gift.

Every year during the Christmas season, my mom baked biscotti, but I never tried them. Christmas was a time when most of Mom's rules for sweets went out the window, and I think I was too excited to indulge in other holiday cookies that I'd waited for all year long. Plus, biscotti are an adult kind of cookie. It wasn't until I opened Dessert'D that I started baking them myself. I realized that our high altitude and dry climate offer the perfect conditions for baking and storing biscotti, and I've been creating new flavors ever since. If you've been timid about making or eating biscotti in the past, I promise you that these recipes will change your mind.

Tips and Tricks

Biscotti can be made with little effort. They don't have to be perfect, they look best when they are rustic, and you don't need a lot of special tools.

Mixing

The first step in making biscotti is mixing the butter and sugars together. I prefer to do this in my stand mixer with a paddle attachment, but you do not need a mixer to make any of the biscotti in this book. You can get the job done with a large mixing bowl and wooden spoon or spatula.

When you're mixing the butter and sugars together, the main thing you want to accomplish is to make sure there are no chunks of butter. This is where having softened butter is key. The butter should be at room temperature—soft enough that if you spread it onto a piece of warm bread, it wouldn't break the bread.

Forming

Making biscotti requires you to form the cookie dough into a rectangle—or sometimes a circle, as with the Chocolate Brownie Walnut Biscotti (page 80)—before baking it. The rectangle or circle should be an even thickness throughout so that it will bake evenly and then be easier to cut into pieces.

Resting

When the biscotti "loaf" comes out of the oven after the first baking, it's best to let it rest for about 10 minutes before cutting it into pieces. If you cut the biscotti when the loaf is hot, it's more likely to tear, resulting in uneven, ragged pieces.

Cutting

Use a sharp knife, and cut the loaf into pieces that are all the same size so they'll cook evenly during the second baking.

Dipping

Who doesn't like biscotti dipped in chocolate? I call to temper the chocolate, which will give it a beautiful shiny finish and will keep it from being sticky, though this

step is not required. If you plan to give biscotti as a gift or take some to a party, tempering the chocolate would be worth it. Otherwise it's fine to skip this step. If you don't have much time, you can even drizzle the chocolate over the tops instead of dipping.

Storing

Biscotti are dry and crunchy. That's why they're so perfect for dipping in milk, tea, or hot cocoa. I've even dipped biscotti in fro-yo. But in a humid climate, biscotti can become soggy pretty quickly if left out. I suggest you store them in an airtight container at room temperature or in the refrigerator.

I'm a sucker for sweet almond-flavored things. One of the "treats" I ate as a child was dry cereal with almonds because we always had it in the house. These biscotti remind me of that crunchy almond cereal, but they are a little sweeter, and dipping one in milk makes it even better.

Makes 12

$3/4$ cup (170 grams) cane sugar, plus 2 tablespoons for topping

$1/2$ cup (113 grams) salted butter, softened

2 tablespoons packed dark brown sugar

1 tablespoon almond flavor

2 large eggs

$2\,1/4$ cups (284 grams) all-purpose flour

$1/2$ teaspoon baking soda

$1/2$ teaspoon fine sea salt

1 cup (113 grams) sliced almonds with their skins

Preheat the oven to 350°F. Line a cookie sheet with parchment paper.

In the bowl of a stand mixer fitted with the paddle attachment, add $3/4$ cup of the cane sugar, the butter, dark brown sugar, and almond flavor. Mix on low until combined and there are no chunks of butter.

Add the eggs and mix slightly, enough to break the yolks.

In a separate bowl, whisk together the flour, baking soda, and sea salt.

Add the flour mixture to the butter mixture, and mix on low until a stiff dough forms. Add the almonds, and mix again on low to fully incorporate.

Using your hands, form the dough into a 13 x 4-inch rectangle, and place it on the prepared baking sheet. Sprinkle with the remaining 2 tablespoons cane sugar.

Bake for 35 minutes, or until the center looks set but not completely done. Remove from the oven, and let rest on the cookie sheet for 10 minutes.

To cut the biscotti, trim off the short ends of the loaf, and cut the rest into 12 slices. Space 1 inch apart on the cookie sheet and bake for 20 minutes, or until golden-brown, crackled on top, and completely crispy. (You can bake off the little edges for extra snacks.) Let cool completely on the cookie sheet.

Store in an airtight container at room temperature for up to 7 days.

>>> GLUTEN-FREE—REPLACE THE ALL-PURPOSE FLOUR WITH $1\,3/4$ CUPS PLUS 3 TABLESPOONS (297 GRAMS) GLUTEN-FREE FLOUR BLEND.

>>> HIGH ALTITUDE—BAKE THE LOAF AT 350°F FOR 30 MINUTES, OR UNTIL THE CENTER LOOKS SET BUT NOT COMPLETELY DONE. LET REST FOR 10 MINUTES. CUT AS INSTRUCTED, AND BAKE THE BISCOTTI AGAIN FOR 15 MINUTES, OR UNTIL GOLDEN-BROWN, CRACKLED ON TOP, AND COMPLETELY CRISPY.

I found my love of the pairing of lemon with pistachios when Delaney and I first started dating. After a dinner out, I'd always ask to stop for fro-yo. I could never choose between pistachio and lemon, so I'd get both, despite the fact that Delaney would look at me weird. And you know I loved it, because I didn't care that my brand-new boyfriend who I was crazy about thought it was odd.

Makes 12

$3/4$ cup (170 grams) cane sugar, plus 2 tablespoons for topping

$1/2$ cup (113 grams) salted butter, softened

2 teaspoons lemon flavor

2 large eggs

2 cups (255 grams) all-purpose flour

$1^1/2$ teaspoons baking powder

$1/2$ teaspoon fine sea salt

$3/4$ cup (106 grams) roasted, salted, shelled pistachios, finely chopped

Preheat the oven to 350°F. Line a cookie sheet with parchment paper.

In the bowl of a stand mixer fitted with the paddle attachment, add $3/4$ cup of the cane sugar, the butter, and the lemon flavor. Mix on low until combined and there are no chunks of butter.

Add the eggs and mix slightly, enough to break the yolks.

In a separate bowl, whisk together the flour, baking powder, and sea salt.

Add the flour mixture to the butter mixture, and mix on low until a smooth dough forms. Add the pistachios, and mix on low until combined.

Using your hands, form the dough into a 13 x 4-inch rectangle, and place it on the prepared cookie sheet. Sprinkle with the remaining 2 tablespoons cane sugar.

Bake for 35 minutes, or until the center looks set but not completely done. Remove from the oven, and let rest on the cookie sheet for 10 minutes.

To cut the biscotti, trim off the short ends of the loaf, and cut the rest into 12 slices. Space 1 inch apart on the cookie sheet and bake for 20 minutes, or until golden-brown, crackled on top, and completely crispy. (You can bake off the little edges for extra snacks.) Let cool completely on the cookie sheet.

Store in an airtight container at room temperature for up to 7 days.

>>> GLUTEN-FREE—REPLACE THE ALL-PURPOSE FLOUR WITH 1³/₄ CUPS (269 GRAMS) GLUTEN-FREE FLOUR BLEND.

>>> HIGH ALTITUDE—BAKE THE LOAF AT 350°F FOR 30 MINUTES, OR UNTIL THE CENTER LOOKS SET BUT NOT COMPLETELY DONE. REMOVE FROM THE OVEN, AND LET REST ON THE COOKIE SHEET FOR 10 MINUTES. CUT AS INSTRUCTED, AND BAKE THE BISCOTTI FOR 15 MINUTES, OR UNTIL GOLDEN-BROWN, CRACKLED ON TOP, AND COMPLETELY CRISPY.

CHOCOLATE BROWNIE WALNUT BISCOTTI

I get a lot of pleasure out of turning ordinary things into something new and interesting, and this biscotti recipe is a perfect example. Chocolate walnut brownies are pretty common, but triangle-shaped Chocolate Brownie Walnut Biscotti are not.

Makes 12

3/4 cup (170 grams) cane sugar, plus 2 tablespoons for topping

1/2 cup (113 grams) salted butter, softened

2 large eggs

1 1/2 cups plus 1 tablespoon (198 grams) all-purpose flour

1/2 cup plus 3 tablespoons (57 grams) Dutch cocoa powder, sifted

3/4 teaspoon ground vanilla bean

1 1/2 teaspoons baking powder

1/2 teaspoon fine sea salt

3/4 cup (142 grams) semisweet chocolate chips

Heaping 1/2 cup (70 grams) chopped walnuts

Preheat the oven to 350°F. Line a cookie sheet with parchment paper.

In the bowl of a stand mixer fitted with the paddle attachment, add 3/4 cup of the cane sugar and the butter. Mix on low until combined and there are no chunks of butter.

Add the eggs and mix slightly, enough to break the yolks.

In a separate bowl, whisk together the flour, cocoa, vanilla bean, baking powder, and sea salt.

Add the flour mixture to the butter mixture, and mix on low until a smooth dough forms. Add the chocolate chips and walnuts, and mix on low until combined.

Divide the dough in half and, using your hands, form each piece of dough into a disk that is about 5 1/2 inches in diameter. Place the disks on the prepared cookie sheet. Sprinkle each disk with 1 tablespoon of the remaining cane sugar.

Bake for 35 minutes, or until the center of each disk looks set but not completely done. Remove from the oven and let rest on the cookie sheet for 10 minutes.

Cut each disk into 6 wedges, like a pizza. Space the wedges 1 inch apart and bake for 20 minutes, or until crackled on top and completely crispy. Let cool completely on the cookie sheet.

Store in an airtight container at room temperature for up to 7 days.

>>> GLUTEN-FREE—REPLACE THE ALL-PURPOSE FLOUR WITH 1 1/3 CUPS (212 GRAMS) GLUTEN-FREE FLOUR BLEND.

>>> HIGH ALTITUDE—BAKE THE DISKS AT 350°F FOR 30 MINUTES, OR UNTIL THEIR CENTERS LOOK SET BUT NOT COMPLETELY DONE. REMOVE FROM THE OVEN, AND LET REST ON THE COOKIE SHEET FOR 10 MINUTES. CUT AS INSTRUCTED, AND BAKE THE WEDGES FOR ANOTHER 15 MINUTES, OR UNTIL CRACKLED ON TOP AND COMPLETELY CRISPY.

Early on I created a cookie called Positively PB, and over time it morphed into this biscotti recipe. I have a special place in my heart for this recipe, because it takes me back to when I really fell in love with baking and creating new recipes.

Makes 12

½ cup (113 grams) salted butter, softened

½ cup (113 grams) cane sugar, plus 2 tablespoons for topping

½ cup (113 grams) packed dark brown sugar

1 teaspoon vanilla extract

2 large eggs

¾ cup plus 1 tablespoon (227 grams) peanut butter

1½ cups (191 grams) all-purpose flour

½ teaspoon baking soda

½ teaspoon fine sea salt

⅔ cup (131 grams) peanut butter chips

½ cup (65 grams) dried cranberries

Preheat the oven to 350°F. Line a cookie sheet with parchment paper.

In the bowl of a stand mixer fitted with the paddle attachment, add the butter, ½ cup of the cane sugar, dark brown sugar, and vanilla extract. Mix on low until combined and there are no chunks of butter.

Add the eggs and peanut butter to the butter mixture, and mix for 1 to 2 rotations, only enough to break the yolks.

In a separate bowl, whisk together the flour, baking soda, and sea salt.

Add the flour mixture to the butter mixture, and mix on low until almost combined (you'll still see bits of flour—that's okay). Do not overmix. Add the peanut butter chips and cranberries, and mix on low until combined and you no longer see flour. Be careful not to overmix.

Using your hands, form the dough into a 13 x 4-inch rectangle, and place it on the prepared cookie sheet. Sprinkle with the remaining 2 tablespoons cane sugar.

Bake for 35 minutes, or until the center looks set but not completely done. Remove from the oven, and let rest on the cookie sheet for 10 minutes.

To cut the biscotti, trim off just enough from the ends of the loaf to create straight, tidy edges. Cut the loaf in half lengthwise, then cut each half into 6 squares. Space the squares 1 inch apart on the cookie sheet and bake for 20 minutes, or until golden-brown, crackled on top, and completely crispy. (You can bake off the little edges for extra snacks.) Let cool completely on the cookie sheet.

Store in an airtight container at room temperature for up to 7 days.

>>> GLUTEN-FREE—REPLACE THE ALL-PURPOSE FLOUR WITH 1¹/₄ CUPS PLUS 1 TABLESPOON (205 GRAMS) GLUTEN-FREE FLOUR BLEND.

>>> HIGH ALTITUDE—BAKE THE LOAF AT 350°F FOR 30 MINUTES, OR UNTIL THE CENTER LOOKS SET BUT NOT COMPLETELY DONE. REMOVE FROM THE OVEN AND LET REST ON THE COOKIE SHEET FOR 10 MINUTES. CUT AS INSTRUCTED, AND BAKE THE BISCOTTI FOR 15 MINUTES, OR UNTIL GOLDEN-BROWN, CRACKLED ON TOP, AND COMPLETELY CRISPY.

SNICKERDOODLE PECAN BISCOTTI

This biscotti is a nod toward cinnamon-and-sugar-coated cereal. It's very light, thanks to the pecans replacing some of the flour. I think it's absolutely perfect for dipping in milk because it soaks up the liquid, just like cereal does, becoming softer while retaining a crunch.

Makes 12

DOUGH

Scant 1 cup (120 grams) pecans

1½ cups (191 grams) all-purpose flour

½ teaspoon cinnamon

1½ teaspoons baking powder

½ teaspoon fine sea salt

¾ cup (170 grams) cane sugar

½ cup (113 grams) salted butter, softened

1 teaspoon vanilla extract

2 large eggs

TOPPING

2 tablespoons cane sugar

1 teaspoon cinnamon

Preheat the oven to 350°F. Line a cookie sheet with parchment paper.

To make the dough: Place the pecans in the bowl of a food processor, and process for 15 to 20 seconds until they are finely ground and look dry. Do not overprocess or the nuts will turn into a paste. Transfer to a medium bowl.

Add the flour, cinnamon, baking powder, and sea salt to the pecans, and whisk together. Set aside.

In the bowl of a stand mixer fitted with the paddle attachment, add the cane sugar, butter, and vanilla extract. Mix on low until combined and there are no chunks of butter.

Add the eggs and the flour mixture to the butter mixture, and mix on low until a smooth dough forms.

To make the topping: In a small dish, mix together the cane sugar and cinnamon. Set aside.

Using your hands, form the dough into a 13 x 4-inch rectangle, and place it on the prepared cookie sheet. Sprinkle the cinnamon-sugar mixture over the top, and rub it all over the sides of the rectangle.

Bake for 35 minutes, or until the center looks set but not completely done. Remove from the oven, and let rest on the cookie sheet for 10 minutes.

To cut the biscotti, trim off the short ends of the loaf, and cut the rest into 12 slices. Space 1 inch apart and bake for 20 minutes, or until golden-brown, crackled on top, and completely crispy. (You can bake off the little edges for extra snacks.) Let cool completely on the cookie sheet.

Store in an airtight container at room temperature for up to 7 days.

>>> GLUTEN-FREE—REPLACE THE ALL-PURPOSE FLOUR WITH $1\frac{1}{4}$ CUPS PLUS 1 TABLESPOON (205 GRAMS) GLUTEN-FREE FLOUR BLEND.

>>> HIGH ALTITUDE—BAKE THE LOAF AT 350°F FOR 30 MINUTES, OR UNTIL THE CENTER LOOKS SET BUT NOT COMPLETELY DONE. REMOVE FROM THE OVEN AND LET REST ON THE COOKIE SHEET FOR 10 MINUTES. CUT AS INSTRUCTED, AND BAKE THE BISCOTTI FOR 15 MINUTES, OR UNTIL GOLDEN-BROWN, CRACKLED ON TOP, AND COMPLETELY CRISPY.

Biscotti are usually made in traditional flavors, or what I like to think of as serious flavors—almond, vanilla, nuts. At Christmas my mom always made chocolate or spiced biscotti. To break out of the box, I created this recipe just for the fun of it. These are the most colorful biscotti I've ever seen.

Makes 12

DOUGH

¹/₂ cup (113 grams) salted butter, softened

¹/₄ cup plus 2 tablespoons (85 grams) cane sugar

¹/₂ cup plus 1 tablespoon plus 2 teaspoons (85 grams) powdered sugar, sifted

2 teaspoons vanilla extract

2 large eggs

2¹/₂ cups plus 3 tablespoons (340 grams) all-purpose flour

¹/₂ cup (85 grams) rainbow sprinkles

1¹/₂ teaspoons baking powder

¹/₂ teaspoon fine sea salt

GLAZE

1 cup plus 3 tablespoons (170 grams) powdered sugar, sifted

2 tablespoons milk

Preheat the oven to 350°F. Line a cookie sheet with parchment paper.

To make the dough: In the bowl of a stand mixer fitted with the paddle attachment, add the butter, cane sugar, powdered sugar, and vanilla extract. Mix on low until combined and there are no chunks of butter.

Add the eggs and mix slightly, enough to break the yolks.

In a separate bowl, whisk together the flour, rainbow sprinkles, baking powder, and sea salt.

Add the flour mixture to the butter mixture, and mix on low until a smooth dough forms.

Using your hands, form the dough into a 13 x 4-inch rectangle, and place it on the prepared cookie sheet.

Bake for 35 minutes, or until the center looks set but not completely done. Remove from the oven and let rest on the cookie sheet for 10 minutes.

To cut the biscotti, trim off the short ends of the loaf, and cut the rest into 12 slices. Space 1 inch apart on the cookie sheet and bake for 20 minutes, or until golden-brown, crackled on top, and completely crispy. (You can bake off the little edges for extra snacks.) Let cool completely on the cookie sheet.

To make the glaze: In a medium bowl, whisk together the powdered sugar and milk until smooth. Using a spoon, drizzle

(continues)

the glaze over the top of the biscotti. Cover the biscotti and let the glaze set for at least 24 hours before serving or stacking the biscotti.

Store in an airtight container at room temperature for up to 7 days.

>>> GLUTEN-FREE—REPLACE THE ALL-PURPOSE FLOUR WITH 2$\frac{1}{4}$ CUPS PLUS 1 TEASPOON (354 GRAMS) GLUTEN-FREE FLOUR BLEND.

>>> HIGH ALTITUDE—BAKE THE LOAF AT 350°F FOR 30 MINUTES, OR UNTIL THE CENTER LOOKS SET BUT NOT COMPLETELY DONE. REMOVE FROM THE OVEN AND LET REST FOR 10 MINUTES. CUT AS INSTRUCTED, AND BAKE THE BISCOTTI FOR 15 MINUTES, OR UNTIL GOLDEN-BROWN, CRACKLED ON TOP, AND COMPLETELY CRISPY.

When you are a baker you naturally tend to bake things for others; it's part of the fun and love that goes into your craft. I know that Delaney loves caramel anything, and he also loves dipping desserts in his coffee and milk, so I created these Caramel Biscotti especially for him.

Makes 12

DOUGH

6 (85 grams total) Caramel Candies (page 250)

$\frac{1}{2}$ cup (113 grams) salted butter, softened

$\frac{1}{4}$ cup plus 1 tablespoon (71 grams) cane sugar

$\frac{1}{4}$ cup plus 1 tablespoon (71 grams) packed dark brown sugar

1 teaspoon vanilla extract

2 large eggs

2$\frac{1}{4}$ cups plus 3 tablespoons (312 grams) all-purpose flour

$\frac{1}{2}$ teaspoon fine sea salt

$\frac{1}{2}$ teaspoon baking soda

GLAZE

1 cup plus 3 tablespoons (170 grams) powdered sugar, sifted

2 tablespoons Caramel Sauce (page 253)

2 tablespoons milk

Preheat the oven to 350°F. Line a cookie sheet with parchment paper.

To make the dough: Place the caramel candies in a microwave-safe bowl, set aside.

In the bowl of a stand mixer fitted with the paddle attachment, add the butter, cane sugar, dark brown sugar, and vanilla extract. Mix on low until combined and there are no chunks of butter.

Add the eggs and mix slightly, enough to break the yolks.

In a separate bowl, whisk together the flour, sea salt, and baking soda.

Add the flour mixture to the butter mixture. Do not mix yet.

Microwave the caramel candies for about 30 seconds or until melted, immediately add them to the butter mixture, and mix on low until a smooth dough forms.

Using your hands, form the dough into a 13 x 4-inch rectangle, and place it on the prepared cookie sheet.

Bake for 35 minutes, or until the center looks set but not completely done. Remove from the oven and let rest on the cookie sheet for 10 minutes.

To cut the biscotti, trim off the short ends of the loaf, and cut the rest into 12 slices. Space 1 inch apart on the cookie sheet and bake for 25 minutes, or until golden-brown, crackled on top, and completely crispy. (You can bake off the little edges for extra snacks.) Let cool completely on the cookie sheet.

(continues)

To make the glaze: In a medium bowl, whisk together the powdered sugar, caramel sauce, and milk until smooth. Using a spoon, drizzle the glaze over the top of the biscotti. Cover the biscotti and let the glaze set for at least 24 hours before serving or stacking the biscotti.

Store in an airtight container at room temperature for up to 7 days.

>>> GLUTEN-FREE—REPLACE THE ALL-PURPOSE FLOUR WITH 2 CUPS PLUS 1 TABLESPOON PLUS 1 TEASPOON (326 GRAMS) GLUTEN-FREE FLOUR BLEND.

>>> HIGH ALTITUDE—BAKE THE LOAF AT 350°F FOR 30 MINUTES, OR UNTIL THE CENTER LOOKS SET BUT NOT COMPLETELY DONE. REMOVE FROM THE OVEN AND LET REST FOR 10 MINUTES. CUT AS INSTRUCTED, AND BAKE THE BISCOTTI FOR 18 MINUTES, OR UNTIL GOLDEN-BROWN, CRACKLED ON TOP, AND COMPLETELY CRISPY.

It's no secret that one of my favorite things in the world is coconut. So of course I make Toasted-Coconut Biscotti. I love the sweetness of the glaze with the delicately browned coconut.

Makes 16

1 cup (226 grams) cane sugar

1/2 cup (113 grams) salted butter, softened

2 teaspoons coconut extract

2 large eggs

2 cups (255 grams) all-purpose flour

2/3 cup (57 grams) unsweetened finely shredded coconut

1 1/2 teaspoons baking powder

1/2 teaspoon fine sea salt

3/4 cup (43 grams) unsweetened wide-flake coconut

Cookie Glaze (page 262)

Preheat the oven to 350°F. Line a cookie sheet with parchment paper.

In the bowl of a stand mixer fitted with the paddle attachment, add the cane sugar, butter, and coconut extract. Mix on low until combined and there are no chunks of butter.

Add the eggs and mix slightly, enough to break the yolks.

In a separate bowl, whisk together the flour, finely shredded coconut, baking powder, and sea salt.

Add the flour mixture to the butter mixture, and mix on low until a dough forms and you don't see any flour bits.

Divide the dough in half. Using your hands, form each piece into a disk that is about 5½ inches in diameter. Place the disks on the prepared cookie sheet.

Bake for 35 minutes, or until the center of each disk looks set but not completely done. Remove from the oven, and let rest on the cookie sheet for 10 minutes.

Cut each disk into 8 wedges, like a pizza. Space the wedges 1 inch apart on the cookie sheet and bake for 20 minutes, or until golden-brown, crackled on top, and completely crispy. Let cool completely on the cookie sheet.

On a cookie sheet lined with parchment paper, spread out the wide-flake coconut and bake for 5 minutes, or until golden-brown and toasted.

Using a butter knife or a small spatula, spread some cookie glaze on top of each biscotto. Sprinkle the toasted coconut over the tops. Cover the biscotti and let the glaze set for at least 24 hours before serving or stacking the biscotti.

Store in an airtight container at room temperature for up to 7 days.

>>> GLUTEN-FREE—REPLACE THE ALL-PURPOSE FLOUR WITH 1³/₄ CUPS (269 GRAMS) GLUTEN-FREE FLOUR BLEND.

>>> HIGH ALTITUDE—BAKE THE DISKS AT 350°F FOR 30 MINUTES, OR UNTIL THE CENTER OF EACH DISK LOOKS SET BUT NOT COMPLETELY DONE. REMOVE FROM THE OVEN AND LET REST ON THE COOKIE SHEET FOR 10 MINUTES. CUT AS INSTRUCTED, AND BAKE THE WEDGES FOR 15 MINUTES, OR UNTIL GOLDEN-BROWN, CRACKLED ON TOP, AND COMPLETELY CRISPY.

If you have a chocolate lover in your life, these are the biscotti for them. The combination of cocoa, semisweet chocolate, and milk chocolate is decadent enough, but the chocolate sprinkles on top push it over the edge. You'll want a glass of cold milk with these.

Makes 12

1/2 cup (113 grams) salted butter, softened

1/4 cup plus 2 tablespoons (85 grams) cane sugar

1/4 cup plus 2 tablespoons (85 grams) packed dark brown sugar

2 large eggs

1 2/3 cups (212 grams) all-purpose flour

1/2 cup (43 grams) Dutch cocoa powder, sifted

1/2 teaspoon ground vanilla bean

1 1/2 teaspoons baking powder

1/2 teaspoon fine sea salt

3/4 cup (142 grams) semisweet chocolate chips

Heaping 1 1/2 cups (226 grams) chopped milk chocolate

Chocolate sprinkles

Preheat the oven to 350°F. Line a cookie sheet with parchment paper.

In the bowl of a stand mixer fitted with the paddle attachment, add the butter, cane sugar, and dark brown sugar. Mix on low until combined and there are no chunks of butter.

Add the eggs and mix slightly, enough to break the yolks.

In a separate bowl, whisk together the flour, cocoa, vanilla bean, baking powder, and sea salt.

Add the flour mixture to the butter mixture, and mix on low until a smooth dough forms. Add the chocolate chips, and mix to fully combine.

Using your hands, form the dough into a 13 x 4-inch rectangle, and place it on the prepared cookie sheet.

Bake for 35 minutes, or until the center looks set but not completely done. Remove from the oven and let rest on the cookie sheet for 10 minutes.

To cut the biscotti, trim off the short ends of the loaf, and cut the rest into 12 slices. Space 1 inch apart on the cookie sheet and bake for 20 minutes, or until crackled on top and completely crispy. (You can bake off the little edges for extra snacks.) Let cool completely on the cookie sheet.

Temper the milk chocolate using the technique on page 268.

Dip the long side of each biscotto halfway into the melted chocolate, and return it to the cookie sheet. Top the biscotti with chocolate sprinkles.

Place the cookie sheet in the refrigerator for at least 1 hour, to set the chocolate.

Store in an airtight container at room temperature for up to 7 days.

>>> GLUTEN-FREE—REPLACE THE ALL-PURPOSE FLOUR WITH A SCANT 1$^1/_2$ CUPS (227 GRAMS) GLUTEN-FREE FLOUR BLEND.

>>> HIGH ALTITUDE—BAKE THE LOAF AT 350°F FOR 30 MINUTES, OR UNTIL THE CENTER LOOKS SET BUT NOT COMPLETELY DONE. REMOVE FROM THE OVEN AND LET REST ON THE COOKIE SHEET FOR 10 MINUTES. CUT AS INSTRUCTED, AND BAKE THE BISCOTTI FOR 15 MINUTES, OR UNTIL CRACKLED ON TOP AND COMPLETELY CRISPY.

I decided to cut these biscotti into squares because they reminded me of the little biscuits my mom used to eat with her tea. I would drink tea with her just to get the biscuits.

Makes 10

½ cup (113 grams) salted butter, softened

½ cup (113 grams) cane sugar

¼ cup (57 grams) packed dark brown sugar

1 teaspoon vanilla extract

2 large eggs

2 chai (black) tea bags

2 cups (255 grams) all-purpose flour

½ teaspoon baking soda

½ teaspoon fine sea salt

1¾ cups (284 grams) chopped white chocolate

Preheat the oven to 350°F. Line a cookie sheet with parchment paper.

In the bowl of a stand mixer fitted with the paddle attachment, add the butter, cane sugar, dark brown sugar, and vanilla extract. Mix on low until combined and there are no chunks of butter.

Add the eggs and mix slightly, enough to break the yolks.

Open the tea bags and transfer the contents to a medium bowl. Add the flour, baking soda, and sea salt, and whisk together.

Add the flour mixture to the butter mixture, and mix on low until a smooth dough forms.

Using your hands, form the dough into a 13 x 4-inch rectangle and place it on the prepared cookie sheet.

Bake for 35 minutes, or until the center looks set but not completely done. Remove from the oven and let rest on the cookie sheet for 10 minutes.

To cut the biscotti, trim the ends off the loaf to create straight, tidy edges. Cut the loaf in half lengthwise, then cut each half into 5 squares. Space 1 inch apart on the cookie sheet and bake for 20 minutes, or until golden-brown, crackled on top, and completely crispy. (You can bake off the little edges for extra snacks.) Let cool completely on the cookie sheet.

Temper the white chocolate using the technique on page 268.

Dip each biscotto diagonally into the white chocolate, covering about half the cookie, and return it to the cookie sheet. Place the cookie sheet in the refrigerator for at least 1 hour, to set the chocolate.

Store in an airtight container at room temperature for up to 7 days.

>>> GLUTEN-FREE—REPLACE THE ALL-PURPOSE FLOUR WITH 1 3/4 CUPS (269 GRAMS) GLUTEN-FREE FLOUR BLEND.

>>> HIGH ALTITUDE—BAKE THE LOAF AT 350°F FOR 30 MINUTES, OR UNTIL THE CENTER LOOKS SET BUT NOT COMPLETELY DONE. REMOVE FROM THE OVEN AND LET REST FOR 10 MINUTES. CUT AS INSTRUCTED, AND BAKE THE SQUARES FOR 15 MINUTES, OR UNTIL GOLDEN-BROWN, CRACKLED ON TOP, AND COMPLETELY CRISPY.

This is one of my all-time favorite biscotti recipes. I could eat these for breakfast, lunch, dinner, and, of course, dessert!

Makes 12

½ cup (113 grams) salted butter, softened

½ cup (113 grams) cane sugar, plus 2 tablespoons for topping

2 tablespoons raw honey

1 teaspoon vanilla extract

2 large eggs

2¼ cups (284 grams) all-purpose flour

½ teaspoon baking soda

½ teaspoon fine sea salt, plus more for topping

Heaping 1½ cups (226 grams) chopped milk chocolate

>>> GLUTEN-FREE—REPLACE THE ALL-PURPOSE FLOUR WITH 1¾ CUPS PLUS 3 TABLESPOONS (297 GRAMS) GLUTEN-FREE FLOUR BLEND.

>>> HIGH ALTITUDE—BAKE THE LOAF AT 350°F FOR 30 MINUTES, OR UNTIL THE CENTER LOOKS SET BUT NOT COMPLETELY DONE. REMOVE FROM THE OVEN AND LET REST ON THE COOKIE SHEET FOR 10 MINUTES. CUT AS INSTRUCTED, AND BAKE THE BISCOTTI FOR 15 MINUTES, OR UNTIL GOLDEN-BROWN, CRACKLED ON TOP, AND COMPLETELY CRISPY.

Preheat the oven to 350°F. Line a cookie sheet with parchment paper.

In the bowl of a stand mixer fitted with the paddle attachment, add the butter, ½ cup of the cane sugar, honey, and vanilla extract. Mix on low until combined and there are no chunks of butter.

Add the eggs and mix slightly, enough to break the yolks.

In a separate bowl, whisk together the flour, baking soda, and ½ teaspoon of the sea salt.

Add the flour mixture to the butter mixture, and mix on low until a smooth dough forms.

Using your hands, form the dough into a 13 x 4-inch rectangle and place it on the prepared cookie sheet. Sprinkle with the remaining 2 tablespoons cane sugar.

Bake for 35 minutes, or until the center looks set but not completely done. Remove from the oven and let rest on the cookie sheet for 10 minutes.

To cut the biscotti, trim off the short ends of the loaf, and cut the rest into 12 slices. Space 1 inch apart on the cookie sheet and bake for 20 minutes, or until golden-brown, crackled on top, and completely crispy. (You can bake off the little edges for extra snacks.) Let cool completely on the cookie sheet.

Temper the milk chocolate using the technique on page 268.

Dip the long side of each biscotto halfway into the melted chocolate and return it to the cookie sheet. Place the cookie sheet in the refrigerator for at least 1 hour, to set the chocolate.

Sprinkle sea salt on top of the set chocolate.

Store in an airtight container at room temperature for up to 7 days.

BUTTER COOKIES

LOTS OF DIFFERENT CULTURES HAVE THEIR OWN VERSION of butter cookies. The Greeks, for example, have two kinds of butter cookies that are traditionally served around Christmas. I am part Greek and grew up eating both of these cookies throughout my childhood. I've included my favorite, YiaYia Cookies (page 124), in this chapter. When I was young, my dad received Danish butter cookies as a Christmas gift from one of his business associates. When he walked in the door with that small blue tin under his arm, I couldn't wait to open it, and I'd stare at all the different-shaped cookies in their perfect little rows. They were so pretty I had a hard time choosing which one I was going to eat, though I'd eventually try them all.

All butter cookies have one main thing in common—yes, butter! And lots of it, compared to most other cookies. These classic cookies are usually made with only a few ingredients: butter, sugar, and flour. Because butter cookies have a dense, crispy texture, there is no need for a leavening agent such as baking soda or baking powder. That means they're really simple to make. You probably even have the ingredients on hand already.

Butter cookies come in all shapes and sizes. They can be piped with a fancy tip, scooped with a cookie scoop, or rolled by hand, which is my personal favorite way to prepare them, probably because I am really fast at this technique from baking so many at Dessert'D.

Sometimes butter cookies need to be refrigerated before going into the oven, and sometimes they do not—be sure to read the recipe closely. You can place them close together on the cookie sheet because they hold their shape and don't spread out when baking. Their sweet, buttery flavor makes them the perfect blank canvas for adding lots of different flavors, though I think they taste amazing on their own.

Tips and Tricks

Butter

When butter is the main ingredient, it's really important to pay attention to how you use it. If the ingredient list says, "butter, softened," that means lightly pressing your finger into the butter should leave an indentation. If the butter is not soft enough, you risk overmixing the dough (to sufficiently cream the hard butter with the sugar), which will make the cookies tough. When a recipe says to use cold butter, as it does for the Strawberry Thumbprints (page 128), make sure the butter comes straight from the refrigerator. Using warmer butter will change the texture of the finished cookie—and not for the better.

Mixing

The shortbread and YiaYia Cookie recipes call to mix the dough until smooth. It should feel like play dough in your hands, and you shouldn't be able to see any chunks of butter. Dough that is improperly mixed will cause holes to form in the bottom of the cookies, which will develop an airy texture instead of a crisp, dense, buttery crumb, which is what you are looking for in a butter cookie. If you are making Spritz Cookies (page 122), I highly recommend using a timer while mixing the dough; it's easy to forget how much time has gone by when you have a 5-minute mix time.

Gluten-Free

In previous chapters you probably noticed that to switch the recipe to gluten-free you just needed a gluten-free flour blend. Because butter cookies have so few ingredients, those ingredients really matter, and each one plays a huge role. Gluten helps dough rise, and it gives baked goods a chewy texture, but in butter cookies gluten is also responsible for the nice crumb. That's why I've brought in coconut flour to the rescue. Coconut flour is drier than other flours, and when you use it along with a gluten-free flour blend, it helps give butter cookies their nice, crispy texture—just like their gluten-filled friends. Remember, though, that gluten-free cookies won't brown as much as those that use all-purpose flour. Watch carefully to make sure they don't burn.

Storing

It's best to store all butter cookies in an airtight container at room temperature. But if you live in a dry climate, you can usually leave them out with no problems. If they are dipped or covered in chocolate, and it's hotter than usual, store them in the refrigerator.

I'll admit it: after I created these cookies it was game over. I eat them almost daily. I have a bag of them in my purse at all times, in my lunch bag, on my desk, and in my pantry. Delaney used to ask me why I had so many bags stashed everywhere, but after he tasted them he started going straight to the closest hiding place and eating them himself.

Makes 40 to 45

¹/₄ cup plus 2 tablespoons (85 grams) coconut oil

¹/₄ cup plus 1 tablespoon (71 grams) cane sugar

¹/₄ cup plus 1 tablespoon (71 grams) packed dark brown sugar

2 teaspoons vanilla extract

¹/₂ cup (113 grams) salted butter, softened

2¹/₄ cups (284 grams) all-purpose flour

¹/₂ teaspoon fine sea salt

³/₄ cup (142 grams) semisweet chocolate chips

Preheat the oven to 350°F. Line 2 cookie sheets with parchment paper.

In the bowl of a stand mixer fitted with the paddle attachment, add the coconut oil, cane sugar, dark brown sugar, and vanilla extract. Mix on low until combined and there are no chunks of coconut oil.

Add the butter, and mix just until the butter has broken up; you will still see chunks of butter.

In a separate bowl, whisk together the flour and sea salt. Add the flour mixture and the chocolate chips to the butter mixture, and mix on low until combined into a dough.

Using a 1.3-ounce cookie scoop, scoop dough onto the prepared cookie sheets (20 to 23 should fit on each cookie sheet). Space the balls about 1 inch apart. Flatten each ball slightly.

Bake for 16 minutes, or until the cookies are lightly browned. Let cool completely on the cookie sheets.

Store in an airtight container at room temperature for up to 10 days.

>>> GLUTEN-FREE—REPLACE THE ALL-PURPOSE FLOUR WITH A SCANT 1¹/₂ CUPS (226 GRAMS) GLUTEN-FREE FLOUR BLEND AND A SCANT ¹/₂ CUP (43 GRAMS) COCONUT FLOUR.

>>> HIGH ALTITUDE—BAKE AT 350°F FOR 15 MINUTES, OR UNTIL THE COOKIES ARE LIGHTLY BROWNED.

Once I made my first batch of mini cookies, I knew I had to develop more flavors because they were so good. And the adorable small size makes them perfect for snacking, sharing, and serving at parties. These have a little something extra: they are dipped in dark chocolate. For the best flavor, buy Jem Organics sprouted, stone-ground chocolate hazelnut butter.

Makes 50

1/4 cup plus 2 tablespoons (85 grams) coconut oil

1/4 cup plus 2 tablespoons (85 grams) packed dark brown sugar

1/4 cup (57 grams) cane sugar

1 1/2 teaspoons vanilla extract

2/3 cup (142 grams) chocolate hazelnut butter

1/2 cup (113 grams) salted butter, softened

2 1/2 cups (318 grams) all-purpose flour

1/3 cup (28 grams) Dutch cocoa powder, sifted

1/2 teaspoon fine sea salt

1 cup (142 grams) finely chopped dark chocolate

Preheat the oven to 350°F. Line 2 cookie sheets with parchment paper.

In the bowl of a stand mixer fitted with the paddle attachment, add the coconut oil, dark brown sugar, cane sugar, and vanilla extract. Mix on low until combined and there are no chunks of coconut oil.

Add the chocolate hazelnut butter and the butter, and mix just until the butter has broken up; you will still see chunks of butter.

In a separate bowl, whisk together the flour, cocoa, and sea salt. Add to the butter mixture, and mix on low until a smooth dough forms.

Using a 1.3-ounce cookie scoop, scoop the dough onto the prepared cookie sheets (25 should fit on each cookie sheet). Space them about 1 inch apart. Flatten each ball slightly.

Bake for 16 minutes, or until the edges appear set and mostly dry. Let cool completely on the cookie sheets.

Temper the dark chocolate using the technique on page 268.

Dip each cookie halfway into the melted chocolate, and return it to the cookie sheet. Place the cookie sheets in the refrigerator for at least 1 hour, to set the chocolate.

Store in an airtight container at room temperature for up to 10 days.

>>> GLUTEN-FREE—REPLACE THE ALL-PURPOSE FLOUR WITH 1 3/4 CUPS PLUS 1 TABLESPOON (276 GRAMS) GLUTEN-FREE FLOUR BLEND AND A SCANT 1/2 CUP (43 GRAMS) COCONUT FLOUR.

>>> HIGH ALTITUDE—BAKE AT 350°F FOR 15 MINUTES, OR UNTIL THE EDGES APPEAR SET AND MOSTLY DRY.

When I first opened Dessert'D I didn't have anything with rainbow sprinkles on the menu, but I got a lot of requests for them. I knew I had to find a better option than the sprinkles made with artificial colors and flavors that didn't even taste good. Then I found India Tree's Nature's Colors Sprinkles, and I created this recipe. They became so popular that we now bake them every day.

Makes 36

1 cup (226 grams) salted butter, softened

1 cup (142 grams) powdered sugar, sifted

1 tablespoon vanilla extract

2 cups (255 grams) all-purpose flour

2/3 cup (113 grams) rainbow or chocolate sprinkles

Preheat the oven to 350°F. Line 2 cookie sheets with parchment paper.

In the bowl of a stand mixer fitted with the paddle attachment, add the butter, powdered sugar, and vanilla extract. Mix on low until you no longer see powdered sugar. There should still be chunks of butter; do not overmix.

Add the flour, and mix on low until combined into a smooth dough; it should feel like play dough in your hands.

Pour the sprinkles into a small dish. Set aside.

Using your hands, form the dough into 36 balls and place them on the prepared cookie sheets about 1 inch apart (18 should fit on each cookie sheet). Flatten each ball slightly. They should look like disks that are about 1¾ inches in diameter.

Dip the top of each disk in the sprinkles, and return it to the cookie sheet.

Bake for 13 minutes, or until lightly browned on the bottom. Let cool completely on the cookie sheets.

Store in an airtight container at room temperature for up to 7 days.

>>> GLUTEN-FREE—REPLACE THE ALL-PURPOSE FLOUR WITH A SCANT 1½ CUPS (226 GRAMS) GLUTEN-FREE FLOUR BLEND AND ½ CUP PLUS 1 TABLESPOON (57 GRAMS) COCONUT FLOUR.

>>> HIGH ALTITUDE—BAKE AT 350°F FOR 12 MINUTES, OR UNTIL LIGHTLY BROWNED ON THE BOTTOM.

COCONUT SHORTBREAD

Sometimes the simplest flavors are the best. Rich butter and sweet coconut—I need nothing else in life.

Makes 36

1 cup (226 grams) salted butter, softened

1 cup (142 grams) powdered sugar, sifted

1 tablespoon vanilla extract

1 teaspoon coconut extract

2 cups (255 grams) all-purpose flour

1 cup (85 grams) unsweetened finely shredded coconut

Preheat the oven to 350°F. Line 2 cookie sheets with parchment paper.

In the bowl of a stand mixer fitted with the paddle attachment, add the butter, powdered sugar, vanilla extract, and coconut extract. Mix on low until you no longer see powdered sugar. There should still be chunks of butter; do not overmix.

Add the flour and coconut, and mix on low until combined into a smooth dough; it should feel like play dough in your hands.

Using your hands, form the dough into 36 balls and place them on the prepared cookie sheets, leaving 1 inch between them (18 should fit on each cookie sheet). Flatten each ball slightly. They should look like disks that are about 1¾ inches in diameter.

Bake for 13 minutes, or until lightly browned on the bottom. Let cool completely on the cookie sheets.

Store in an airtight container at room temperature for up to 7 days.

>>> GLUTEN-FREE—REPLACE THE ALL-PURPOSE FLOUR WITH A SCANT 1½ CUPS (226 GRAMS) GLUTEN-FREE FLOUR BLEND AND ½ CUP PLUS 1 TABLESPOON (57 GRAMS) COCONUT FLOUR.

>>> HIGH ALTITUDE—BAKE AT 350°F FOR 12 MINUTES, OR UNTIL LIGHTLY BROWNED ON THE BOTTOM.

When the weather is cool and crisp and the leaves are changing, I crave sweet and spicy cookies. The spices in these cookies just scream fall to me. I love that they aren't too sweet, so when you add a drizzle of glaze the result is perfect cookie harmony.

Makes 36

DOUGH

1 cup (226 grams) salted butter, softened

1 cup (142 grams) powdered sugar, sifted

1 tablespoon vanilla extract

2 cups (255 grams) all-purpose flour

1 teaspoon cinnamon

$1/2$ teaspoon ginger

$1/2$ teaspoon allspice

$1/4$ teaspoon cardamom

$1/4$ teaspoon cloves

$1/4$ teaspoon black pepper

GLAZE

1 cup plus 3 tablespoons (170 grams) powdered sugar, sifted

2 tablespoons milk

Preheat the oven to 350°F. Line 2 cookie sheets with parchment paper.

To make the dough: In the bowl of a stand mixer fitted with the paddle attachment, add the butter, powdered sugar, and vanilla extract. Mix on low until you no longer see any powdered sugar. There should still be chunks of butter; do not overmix.

Add the flour, cinnamon, ginger, allspice, cardamom, cloves, and black pepper, and mix on low until a smooth dough forms; it should feel like play dough in your hands.

Using your hands, form the dough into 36 balls and place them on the prepared cookie sheets, leaving 1 inch between them (18 should fit on each cookie sheet). Flatten each ball slightly. They should look like disks that are about 1¾ inches in diameter.

Bake for 13 minutes, or until lightly browned on the bottom. Let cool completely on the cookie sheets.

To make the glaze: In a medium bowl, whisk together the powdered sugar and milk until smooth. Using a spoon, drizzle the glaze over the tops of the cookies. Cover the cookies and let the glaze set for at least 24 hours before serving or stacking the cookies.

Store in an airtight container at room temperature for up to 7 days.

>>> GLUTEN-FREE—REPLACE THE ALL-PURPOSE FLOUR WITH A SCANT 1$1/2$ CUPS (226 GRAMS) GLUTEN-FREE FLOUR BLEND AND $1/2$ CUP PLUS 1 TABLESPOON (57 GRAMS) COCONUT FLOUR.

>>> HIGH ALTITUDE—BAKE AT 350°F FOR 12 MINUTES, OR UNTIL LIGHTLY BROWNED ON THE BOTTOM.

When we moved from Chicago to Michigan my mom thought it would be a good idea for me join Girl Scouts to meet new friends. She signed me up, without my permission, and told me to go to the meetings after school. I attended one meeting, swore to never go again, and instead went to my friend Emily's house just down the street. I'd walk home afterward, pretending I'd been to a scout meeting. When the time came to sell Girl Scout cookies and Mom asked for my cookie-selling form, I knew I was caught. Had I remembered that Girl Scouts sell cookies, I probably would have stuck it out until cookie-selling season. Instead, I ended up buying cookies from my scouting friends. My favorites turned out to be the Thanks-A-Lots, which are similar to these shortbread cookies, but I think my recipe tastes even better. Perhaps if I had been a more patient Girl Scout, I would have started my cookie career a lot sooner.

Makes 36

1 cup (226 grams) salted butter, softened

1 cup (142 grams) powdered sugar, sifted

1 tablespoon almond flavor

1 teaspoon vanilla extract

2 cups (255 grams) all-purpose flour

Heaping 1 1/2 cups (227 grams) finely chopped milk chocolate

Preheat the oven to 350°F. Line 2 cookie sheets with parchment paper.

In the bowl of a stand mixer fitted with the paddle attachment, add the butter, powdered sugar, almond flavor, and vanilla extract. Mix on low until just combined. There should still be chunks of butter; do not overmix.

Add the flour, and mix on low until combined into a smooth dough; it should feel like play dough in your hands.

Using your hands, form the dough into 36 balls and place them on the prepared cookie sheets, leaving 1 inch between them (18 should fit on each cookie sheet). Flatten each ball slightly. They should look like disks that are about 1¾ inches in diameter.

Bake for 13 minutes, or until the edges are golden-brown. Let cool completely on the cookie sheets.

Temper the milk chocolate using the technique on page 268.

Dip the bottom of each cookie into the melted chocolate, and return it, chocolate-side down, to the parchment-lined cookie sheet. Place the cookie sheets in the refrigerator for at least 1 hour, to set the chocolate.

Store in an airtight container at room temperature for up to 7 days.

>>> GLUTEN-FREE—REPLACE THE ALL-PURPOSE FLOUR
WITH A SCANT 1^1/$_2$ CUPS (226 GRAMS) GLUTEN-FREE
FLOUR BLEND AND ^{1}/$_2$ CUP PLUS 1 TABLESPOON (57
GRAMS) COCONUT FLOUR.

>>> HIGH ALTITUDE—BAKE AT 350°F FOR 12 MINUTES,
OR UNTIL THE EDGES ARE GOLDEN-BROWN.

The first bakery I ever worked at made cookies called Crack Butter Cookies. They looked very unassuming, but they soon became my daily snack, along with a glass of chocolate milk. The name truly fits because you can't stop eating these cookies. Even though I never baked them at my first bakery job, once I left I couldn't stop thinking about them. They say imitation is the highest form of flattery, and in this case it is true. It took me what I hope was only about a hundred tries before I finally developed a recipe I was satisfied with. Thank you, Linda, for your mentoring, and for giving me my first job in a bakery. Because eggs can vary so much in size, weighing the egg whites will truly give you the most reliable results here.

Makes 50

2 (56 grams) medium egg whites

1/2 cup (113 grams) salted butter, softened

1/2 cup (113 grams) cane sugar

1/2 teaspoon vanilla extract

1/2 cup (70 grams) cake flour

Preheat the oven to 350°F. Line 3 cookie sheets with parchment paper.

In the bowl of a stand mixer fitted with the whisk attachment, beat the egg whites on low, gradually increasing the speed to high as the whites begin to thicken; continue beating until stiff peaks form. Transfer the beaten whites to a separate bowl. (There's no need to wash the mixing bowl or the whisk for the next step.)

In the same bowl of the stand mixer fitted with the whisk attachment, mix the butter, sugar, and vanilla extract on low until combined and there are no chunks of butter. Add the cake flour, and mix on low until combined.

Remove the bowl from the stand mixer, and, using a rubber spatula, carefully fold the egg whites into the butter mixture until a smooth batter forms.

Insert Ateco tip #804 into a large piping bag, and fill the bag with the cookie batter. Pipe dollops of dough, each about the size of a quarter, onto the prepared cookie sheets, leaving 2 inches between them.

Bake for 12 minutes, or until the edges turn golden-brown. Let cool completely on the cookie sheets.

Store in an airtight container at room temperature for up to 7 days.

>>> GLUTEN-FREE—REPLACE THE CAKE FLOUR WITH $^1/_4$ CUP PLUS 3 TABLESPOONS PLUS 1 TEASPOON (70 GRAMS) GLUTEN-FREE FLOUR BLEND.

>>> HIGH ALTITUDE—BAKE AT 350°F FOR 9 MINUTES, OR UNTIL THE EDGES TURN GOLDEN-BROWN.

When I was young, my mom occasionally bought a bag of Pepperidge Farm Milano mint cookies and hid them from us kids. But I knew where to find them. I loved biting into those forbidden cookies—crisp, buttery, and sweet, with their hint of mint and chocolate. But I always wished they had more chocolate. Flash forward to today, and I have created my own version, which definitely has more chocolate.

Makes 36

1 cup (226 grams) salted butter, softened

1 cup plus 3 tablespoons (170 grams) powdered sugar, sifted

1 tablespoon vanilla extract

2 teaspoons peppermint flavor

1 large egg

1 large egg yolk

2 1/2 cups plus 3 tablespoons (340 grams) all-purpose flour

Heaping 1 1/2 cups (227 grams) finely chopped milk chocolate

>>> GLUTEN-FREE—REPLACE THE ALL-PURPOSE FLOUR WITH 2 CUPS (310 GRAMS) GLUTEN-FREE FLOUR BLEND AND A SCANT 1/2 CUP (43 GRAMS) COCONUT FLOUR.

>>> HIGH ALTITUDE—BAKE AT 350°F FOR 15 MINUTES, OR UNTIL GOLDEN-BROWN ON THE EDGES AND BOTTOM.

Preheat the oven to 350°F. Line 2 cookie sheets with parchment paper.

In the bowl of a stand mixer fitted with the paddle attachment, add the butter, powdered sugar, vanilla extract, and peppermint flavor. Mix on low until combined and there are no chunks of butter.

Add the egg and egg yolk, and mix on low for only a few rotations to combine.

Add the flour, and mix on low until combined into a smooth dough.

Using your hands, form the dough into 36 balls and place them on the prepared cookie sheets about 1 inch apart (18 should fit on each cookie sheet). Flatten each ball slightly. They should look like disks that are about 1¾ inches in diameter.

Refrigerate the cookie sheets for 20 minutes.

Bake for 20 minutes, or until golden-brown on the edges and bottom. Let cool completely on the cookie sheets.

Temper the milk chocolate using the technique on page 268.

Dip the bottom of each cookie into the melted chocolate, and return it, chocolate-side down, to the parchment-lined cookie sheet. Place the cookie sheets in the refrigerator for at least 1 hour, to set the chocolate.

Store in an airtight container at room temperature for up to 7 days.

Spritz Cookies and
Chocolate Espresso
Spritz Cookies

SPRITZ COOKIES

Spritz is a German word that means "to squirt." And that's how you make these cookies: soft dough is pushed (or squirted) through a cookie press to create different shapes. I got to eat these cookies every Christmas courtesy of my best friend and next-door neighbor, Celeste. Like clockwork, the minute we got out of school for Christmas break, their house was stocked with spritz cookies. Celeste and I would sit at her grand dining room table with a plate of those cookies between us while we wrote our Christmas lists and sipped hot cocoa, holiday music playing softly in the background. I always felt like I was in a Christmas movie during that yearly ritual.

Makes 50

1 cup (226 grams) salted butter, softened

³/₄ cup (170 grams) cane sugar

2 teaspoons vanilla extract

¹/₂ teaspoon almond flavor

1 large egg

2 cups (255 grams) all-purpose flour

OPTIONAL GARNISHES

Rainbow sprinkles

Dark chocolate chunks

Strawberry Preserves (page 266)

>>> GLUTEN-FREE—REPLACE THE ALL-PURPOSE FLOUR WITH A SCANT 1¹/₂ CUPS (227 GRAMS) GLUTEN-FREE FLOUR BLEND AND ¹/₂ CUP PLUS 1 TABLESPOON (57 GRAMS) COCONUT FLOUR.

>>> HIGH ALTITUDE—BAKE AT 350°F FOR 10 MINUTES, OR UNTIL GOLDEN-BROWN AROUND THE EDGES.

Preheat the oven to 350°F. Line 2 cookie sheets with parchment paper.

In the bowl of a stand mixer fitted with the paddle attachment, add the butter, cane sugar, vanilla extract, and almond flavor. Mix on low for 5 to 7 minutes, until the mixture is light in color and fluffy.

Add the egg, and mix until combined.

Add the flour, and mix on low until combined into a smooth dough.

Insert Ateco tip #846 into a large piping bag (or use a cookie press if you have one), and fill the bag with half the cookie dough. (If you put it all in at once, it can be too hard to squeeze out.)

Pipe the dough in 1½-inch dollops onto the prepared cookie sheets, leaving 1 inch between them.

If desired, sprinkle the piped dough with rainbow sprinkles, press a chunk of chocolate into the middle, or press your finger into the middle to make an indentation, and fill it with strawberry preserves.

Bake for 13 minutes, or until golden-brown around the edges. Let cool completely on the cookie sheets.

Store in an airtight container at room temperature for up to 7 days.

These cookies have all the flavors you could want: butter, chocolate, coffee, and even more chocolate. And they are so tasty!

Makes 32

2 tablespoons coffee beans

³/₄ cup (95 grams) all-purpose flour

¹/₄ cup (21 grams) Dutch cocoa powder, sifted

¹/₂ cup (113 grams) salted butter, softened

¹/₄ cup plus 2 tablespoons (85 grams) cane sugar

1 teaspoon vanilla extract

1 large egg

Chocolate sprinkles

1¹/₄ cups (185 grams) finely chopped milk chocolate

>>> GLUTEN-FREE—REPLACE THE ALL-PURPOSE FLOUR WITH ¹/₂ CUP (78 GRAMS) GLUTEN-FREE FLOUR BLEND AND ¹/₄ CUP PLUS 1 TABLESPOON (28 GRAMS) COCONUT FLOUR.

>>> HIGH ALTITUDE—BAKE AT 350°F FOR 10 MINUTES, OR UNTIL THE EDGES LOOK SET AND MOSTLY DRY.

Preheat the oven to 350°F. Line 2 cookie sheets with parchment paper.

Using a coffee grinder or a spice grinder, grind the coffee beans into a very fine powder. (If they are not ground all the way to a powder, the cookies may be grainy.) Place the ground coffee in a medium bowl, add the flour and cocoa powder, and whisk together. Set aside.

In the bowl of a stand mixer fitted with the paddle attachment, add the butter, cane sugar, and vanilla extract. Mix on low for 5 to 7 minutes, until the mixture is light in color and fluffy.

Add the egg, and mix until combined.

Add the flour mixture, and mix on low until combined into a smooth dough.

Insert Ateco tip #846 into a large piping bag (or use a cookie press if you have one), and fill the bag with half the cookie dough. (If you put it all in at once, it can be too hard to squeeze out.)

Pipe the dough in 1½-inch dollops onto the prepared cookie sheets, leaving 1 inch between them. Sprinkle the dough with the chocolate sprinkles.

Bake for 13 minutes, or until the edges look set and mostly dry. Let cool completely on the cookie sheets.

Temper the milk chocolate using the technique on page 268.

Dip the bottom of each cookie into the melted chocolate, and return it, chocolate-side down, to the parchment-lined cookie sheet. Place the cookie sheets in the refrigerator for at least 1 hour, to set the chocolate.

Store in an airtight container at room temperature for up to 7 days.

YiaYia (pronounced yī-ya) means "grandma" in Greek. I am one-quarter Greek, thanks to my dad's side of the family, and my YiaYia made traditional Greek cookies called kourambiethes (pronounced kor-um-bī-ethes), which were my favorite cookies when I was little. And not much has changed. My cousins and I could never pronounce kourambiethes, so we just called them YiaYia cookies. She never used a recipe—she just put in "a little of this, a little of that"—and they came out perfectly every single time. I have to thank my mom for the countless times she hovered over YiaYia in the kitchen and wrote down exactly what she did to make her famous cookies. I have been serving this cookie since day one at Dessert'D, and it's still one of our most popular cookies.

Makes 48

2 cups (452 grams) salted butter, softened

1/2 cup (71 grams) powdered sugar, sifted, plus a generous amount more for dusting

2 teaspoons vanilla extract

2 tablespoons Seagram's 7 American Blended Whiskey

1 large egg yolk

5 cups (708 grams) King Arthur Unbleached Cake Flour

1/2 teaspoon fine sea salt

Preheat the oven to 325°F. Line 2 cookie sheets with parchment paper.

In the bowl of a stand mixer fitted with the paddle attachment, add the butter, powdered sugar, vanilla extract, whiskey, and egg yolk. Mix on low until combined but chunks of butter remain visible.

Add the cake flour and sea salt, and mix on low until combined into a smooth dough; it should feel like play dough in your hands.

Using your hands, form the dough into 48 balls and place them close together on the prepared cookie sheets (they won't spread while baking, so 24 should fit on each cookie sheet). Flatten each ball slightly. They should look like disks that are about 2 inches in diameter.

Bake for 22 minutes, or until very lightly browned on the bottom. Let cool completely on the cookie sheets.

Sift powdered sugar generously over the tops of the cookies. Store in an airtight container for up to 2 weeks.

>>> GLUTEN-FREE—REPLACE THE CAKE FLOUR WITH 4 1/2 CUPS PLUS 1 TEASPOON (666 GRAMS) GLUTEN-FREE FLOUR BLEND AND A SCANT 1/2 CUP (43 GRAMS) COCONUT FLOUR.

>>> HIGH ALTITUDE—BAKE AT 325°F FOR 12 MINUTES, OR UNTIL VERY LIGHTLY BROWNED ON THE BOTTOM.

Many of our customers have asked me to bake a lemon-flavored YiaYia cookie, and here it is. As light as the original but with an added citrusy tartness, they have become a great addition to my recipe collection. I think YiaYia would have approved.

Makes 48

2 cups (452 grams) salted butter, softened

1/2 cup (71 grams) powdered sugar, sifted, plus a generous amount more for dusting

1 tablespoon lemon flavor

2 teaspoons vanilla extract

Juice and zest of 1/2 lemon, separated

1 large egg yolk

5 cups (708 grams) King Arthur Unbleached Cake Flour

1/2 teaspoon fine sea salt

Preheat the oven to 325°F. Line 2 cookie sheets with parchment paper.

In the bowl of a stand mixer fitted with the paddle attachment, add the butter, powdered sugar, lemon flavor, vanilla extract, lemon juice, and egg yolk. Mix on low until combined but chunks of butter remain visible.

Add the cake flour, sea salt, and lemon zest, and mix on low until a smooth dough forms; it should feel like play dough in your hands.

Using your hands, form the dough into 48 balls and place them close together on the prepared cookie sheets (they won't spread while baking, so 24 should fit on each cookie sheet). Flatten each ball slightly. They should look like disks that are about 2 inches in diameter.

Bake for 22 minutes, or until very lightly browned on the bottom. Let cool completely on the cookie sheets.

Sift powdered sugar generously over the tops of the cookies. Store in an airtight container for up to 2 weeks.

>>> GLUTEN-FREE—REPLACE THE CAKE FLOUR WITH 4 1/4 CUPS PLUS 1 TEASPOON (666 GRAMS) GLUTEN-FREE FLOUR BLEND AND A SCANT 1/2 CUP (43 GRAMS) COCONUT FLOUR.

>>> HIGH ALTITUDE—BAKE AT 325°F FOR 12 MINUTES, OR UNTIL VERY LIGHTLY BROWNED ON THE BOTTOM.

These little cookies remind me of Pop-Tarts—a breakfast food that was never part of my upbringing. But after we moved from Chicago to Michigan, I had a friend whose dad worked for Kellogg. When I went to her house after school, I got to eat strawberry Pop-Tarts. These cookies remind me of those days. You can eat them warm out of the oven or at room temperature—they are amazing either way.

Makes 30

DOUGH

1 cup (226 grams) cold butter, cut into cubes

1¼ cups plus 2 tablespoons (198 grams) powdered sugar, sifted

1 tablespoon vanilla extract

2¾ cups plus 2 tablespoons (369 grams) all-purpose flour

¼ teaspoon cinnamon

3 tablespoons cane sugar

FILLING

Strawberry Preserves (page 266)

GLAZE

1 cup plus 3 tablespoons (170 grams) powdered sugar, sifted

2 tablespoons milk

Preheat the oven to 350°F. Line 2 cookie sheets with parchment paper.

To make the dough: In the bowl of a stand mixer fitted with the paddle attachment, add the butter, powdered sugar, and vanilla extract. Mix on low until you no longer see powdered sugar; the butter will still be cold and will look a little chunky. Add the flour and cinnamon, and mix on low until the mixture looks like wet sand.

Place the cane sugar in a small bowl; set aside.

Using your hands, form the dough into 30 balls, and arrange them close together on the prepared cookie sheets (15 should fit on each cookie sheet). Roll each ball of dough in the cane sugar, and return it to the cookie sheet. Press your thumb into the center of each ball of dough to form an indentation. Fill it with a dollop of strawberry preserves.

Refrigerate the cookie sheets for 30 minutes.

Bake for 19 minutes, or until lightly browned on the bottom. Let cool completely on the cookie sheets.

To make the glaze: In a medium bowl, whisk together the powdered sugar and milk until smooth. Using a spoon, drizzle the glaze over the tops of the cookies. Cover the cookies and let the glaze set for at least 24 hours before serving or stacking the cookies.

Store in an airtight container at room temperature for up to 7 days.

>>> GLUTEN-FREE—REPLACE THE ALL-PURPOSE FLOUR WITH 2
CUPS (310 GRAMS) GLUTEN-FREE FLOUR BLEND AND $1/2$ CUP PLUS 1
TABLESPOON (57 GRAMS) COCONUT FLOUR.

>>> HIGH ALTITUDE—BAKE AT 350°F FOR 15 MINUTES, OR UNTIL LIGHTLY
BROWNED ON THE BOTTOM.

SANDWICH COOKIES

SANDWICH COOKIES ARE THE BEST because they are actually two cookies in one, plus filling! Buttercream, glaze, whipped cream, caramel, ganache—almost anything can be used to fill a sandwich cookie. And pretty much any cookie can make a sandwich: a soft cookie, a shortbread cookie, a crunchy cookie—whatever you like. In this chapter, you'll find the cookies that I think make the best sandwich cookies.

I remember eating Oreos as a child when my mom allowed it, which was very rarely. But my best friend, Celeste, got to eat them all the time. So most days after school I could be found at Celeste's house eating Oreos. Sometimes we just sat on her kitchen floor, leaning against the fridge and eating them out of the package, and sometimes we dipped them in milk. On occasion, we opened every single cookie to see if we could successfully end up with cream filling on only one side. I don't know why we did this, or why it was a victory if we could do it, but we did, and it was.

Back then I never would have dreamed that I would be baking my very own sandwich cookies for a living. Adding sandwich cookies to the menu came about naturally after I realized how much people love frosting.

Customers were constantly asking for frosted cookies, and since I always want to serve what my customers want, I started to make them, but I wanted them to have a fun twist, like the Snickerdoodle Sandwich Cookies (page 147) and the Neapolitan Sandwich Cookies (page 159) you'll find in this chapter. The great thing about sandwich cookies is that with the frosting on the inside, they are easy to stack on a plate or put in a bag, and they don't stick together. This also makes them perfect for parties, gifts, and storing in your pantry for when your sweet tooth strikes.

Sandwich cookies just evoke fun of all kinds. And they usually combine two flavors into one excessive cookie, creating the ultimate indulgence. I offer two kinds of recipes here: sandwich cookies and cookie pies. The sandwich cookies are crunchy and perfect for dipping in milk. The cookie pies are softer and can be slowly savored as you tear off one piece at a time and let them melt in your mouth. Actually, they are pretty good dunked in milk, too. But the thing to remember is that you can create a sandwich cookie out of any cookie you like—all you need is two cookies and some filling. So go wild, and create the cookie sandwich of your dreams.

Tips and Tricks

Making sandwich cookies is always a two-step operation. You've got to make the cookies first and then the filling. But they are worth waiting for.

Gluten-Free Cookies

All of the sandwich cookies in this chapter can easily be made gluten-free, but they call for two kinds of gluten-free flour, which makes sense because they are butter cookies, and those work better when coconut flour is added to the gluten-free flour blend. Cookie pies are soft and chewy, so a simple gluten-free flour blend will work just fine for them. Remember, you can make gluten-free cookies a little larger than those made with all-purpose flour, because they won't spread or puff up as much.

Filling

Buttercream is my favorite filling for a sandwich cookie. For the best results, be sure to use buttercream that isn't too stiff. If you're making cookie pies, a very stiff buttercream can break or crack the fragile, soft cookies. Also, piping the filling will be more difficult if it's too stiff. If your buttercream seems a bit too stiff, just add a little milk (water also works), 1 teaspoon at a time, mixing thoroughly between additions, until the buttercream is softer. The consistency will depend on the temperature of your butter, so always mix and whip the buttercream *before* adding more liquid. The best thing about buttercream is the fact that it eventually hardens a bit, holding its form in the middle of the cookie, which makes the sandwich easier to eat. You can use lots of other fillings, too. Try filling your cookie sandwiches with Caramel Sauce (page 253) or Butterscotch Sauce (page 249)—delicious!

Sandwiching

Be sure to pair up cookies of the same size. When making homemade cookies, some will turn out a bit larger than others. The best-looking sandwich cookies are made from two cookies of the same size. If you pair them up just before filling them, you'll have as many matched pairs as possible. Sometimes you'll end up with a couple of odd-sized cookies that don't match up well. Consider those the "taster" set—because you need to taste your cookies before serving them to friends, right?

Storing

Cookie pies are best stored in an airtight container to preserve their amazing soft and chewy texture. If you live in a humid climate, you might find that you can leave them out all day with no problem. Sandwich cookies are already crunchy, so they will be okay if you leave them out on a plate on the counter. However, in a humid climate they will become soggy pretty quickly. When in doubt, store them in an airtight container; if it gets hot and humid, put them in the refrigerator. All sandwich cookies can be stored at room temperature for up to 3 days, or in the refrigerator for up to 7 days.

Sometimes you just want the simple pleasure of a vanilla cookie. And these are the perfect base for almost any flavor. Drizzle Butterscotch Sauce (page 249) on top, dip them in Chocolate Milk (page 258) or Strawberry Milk (page 265), or enjoy them with Chocolate Fro-Yo (page 254).

Makes 18 sandwiches

DOUGH

¾ cup (170 grams) cane sugar, plus more for topping

½ cup (113 grams) salted butter, softened

1 teaspoon vanilla extract

2 large eggs

2 cups (255 grams) all-purpose flour

1½ teaspoons baking powder

½ teaspoon fine sea salt

FILLING

1½ cups plus 1 tablespoon (227 grams) powdered sugar, sifted

½ cup (113 grams) salted butter, softened

½ teaspoon ground vanilla bean

1 to 2 teaspoons milk

Preheat the oven to 375°F. Line 2 cookie sheets with parchment paper.

To make the dough: In the bowl of a stand mixer fitted with the paddle attachment, add the cane sugar, butter, and vanilla extract. Mix on low until combined and there are no chunks of butter.

Add the eggs, and mix just slightly.

In a separate bowl, whisk together the flour, baking powder, and sea salt.

Add the flour mixture to the butter mixture, and mix on low until a smooth dough forms.

Using your hands, form the dough into 36 balls, and place them on the prepared cookie sheets about 1 inch apart (18 should fit on each cookie sheet). Flatten them until they are very thin, 2 to 2½ inches in diameter. Once flattened, they can be fairly close together as they won't spread very much while baking.

Bake for 7 minutes, or until lightly browned on the bottom. Sprinkle the tops with cane sugar immediately after they come out of the oven. Let cool completely on the cookie sheets.

To make the filling: In the bowl of a stand mixer fitted with the paddle attachment, add the powdered sugar, butter, vanilla bean, and milk. Mix on low until combined, increase the speed to high, and mix for 1 minute more, or until light and fluffy. Transfer the filling to a piping bag with no tip.

(continues)

Pair the cookies together by size, and turn over every other cookie. Pipe filling onto each turned-over cookie, and sandwich the pairs together.

Store in an airtight container at room temperature for up to 3 days, or in the refrigerator for up to 7 days.

>>> GLUTEN-FREE—REPLACE THE ALL-PURPOSE FLOUR WITH 1$\frac{3}{4}$ CUPS (269 GRAMS) GLUTEN-FREE FLOUR BLEND.

>>> HIGH ALTITUDE—BAKE AT 375°F FOR 5 MINUTES, OR UNTIL LIGHTLY BROWNED ON THE BOTTOM.

One of the forbidden snacks of my childhood was an oatmeal cream pie. Back then, they came individually wrapped in plastic in a white box, and my mom never once bought them. The only way I got to eat them was if a friend had one and I begged them to share. Now these are homemade and I don't have to share.

Makes 18 sandwiches

DOUGH

1/2 cup (113 grams) salted butter, softened

1/4 cup plus 2 tablespoons (85 grams) cane sugar

1/4 cup plus 2 tablespoons (85 grams) packed dark brown sugar

1 teaspoon vanilla extract

2 large eggs

2 cups (255 grams) all-purpose flour

Scant 1 cup (85 grams) rolled oats

2 teaspoons cinnamon

1/2 teaspoon baking soda

1/2 teaspoon fine sea salt

FILLING

1 1/2 cups plus 1 tablespoon (227 grams) powdered sugar, sifted

1/2 cup (113 grams) salted butter, softened

Heaping 1 tablespoon Caramel Sauce (page 253)

Preheat the oven to 375°F. Line 2 cookie sheets with parchment paper.

To make the dough: In the bowl of a stand mixer fitted with the paddle attachment, add the butter, cane sugar, dark brown sugar, and vanilla extract. Mix on low until combined and there are no chunks of butter.

Add the eggs, and mix just slightly.

In a separate bowl, whisk together the flour, oats, cinnamon, baking soda, and sea salt.

Add the flour mixture to the butter mixture, and mix on low until a smooth dough forms.

Using your hands, form the dough into 36 balls and place them on the prepared cookie sheets about 1 inch apart (18 should fit on each cookie sheet). Flatten them until they are very thin, 2 to 2½ inches in diameter. Once flattened, they can be fairly close together as they won't spread very much while baking.

Bake for 7 minutes, or until lightly browned on the bottom. Let cool completely on the cookie sheets.

To make the filling: In the bowl of a stand mixer fitted with the paddle attachment, add the powdered sugar, butter, and caramel sauce. Mix on low until combined, increase the speed to high, and mix for 1 minute more, or until light and fluffy. Transfer the filling to a piping bag with no tip.

Pair the cookies together by size, and turn over every other cookie. Pipe filling onto each turned-over cookie, and sandwich the pairs together.

Store in an airtight container at room temperature for up to 3 days, or in the refrigerator for up to 7 days.

(continues)

>>> GLUTEN-FREE—USE GLUTEN-FREE OATS. REPLACE THE ALL-PURPOSE FLOUR WITH 1³/₄ CUPS (269 GRAMS) GLUTEN-FREE FLOUR BLEND.

>>> HIGH ALTITUDE—BAKE AT 375°F FOR 5 MINUTES, OR UNTIL LIGHTLY BROWNED ON THE BOTTOM.

Pure love. That's pretty much all I have to say about these cookies. I surprised myself when I tasted them the first time—they were that good. If you like peanut butter or butterscotch (or both!), you'll love these cookies, too.

Makes 18 sandwiches

DOUGH

3/4 cup (170 grams) cane sugar, plus more for topping

1/2 cup (113 grams) salted butter, softened

1/4 cup (57 grams) packed dark brown sugar

1 teaspoon vanilla extract

1 large egg

1 large egg yolk

1/2 cup (142 grams) peanut butter

1 1/2 cups (191 grams) all-purpose flour

1/2 teaspoon baking soda

1/2 teaspoon fine sea salt

FILLING

1 1/2 cups plus 1 tablespoon (227 grams) powdered sugar, sifted

1/2 cup (113 grams) salted butter, softened

2 tablespoons Butterscotch Sauce (page 249)

Preheat the oven to 375°F. Line 2 cookie sheets with parchment paper.

To make the dough: In the bowl of a stand mixer fitted with the paddle attachment, add the cane sugar, butter, dark brown sugar, and vanilla extract. Mix on low until combined and there are no chunks of butter.

Add the egg, egg yolk, and peanut butter, and mix for just 2 to 3 rotations. Do not overmix.

In a separate bowl, whisk together the flour, baking soda, and sea salt.

Add the flour mixture to the butter mixture, and mix on low until a smooth dough forms.

Using your hands, form the dough into 36 balls, and place them on the prepared cookie sheets about 1 inch apart (18 should fit on each cookie sheet). Flatten them until they are very thin, 2 to 2½ inches in diameter. Once flattened, they can be fairly close together as they won't spread very much while baking.

Bake for 7 minutes, or until they look set and cracked on top.

Sprinkle the tops with cane sugar immediately after the cookies come out of the oven. Let cool completely on the cookie sheets.

To make the filling: In the bowl of a stand mixer fitted with the paddle attachment, add the powdered sugar, butter, and butterscotch sauce. Mix on low until combined, increase the speed to high, and mix for 1 minute more, or until light and fluffy. Transfer the filling to a piping bag with no tip.

(continues)

Pair the cookies together by size, and turn over every other cookie. Pipe filling onto each turned-over cookie, and sandwich the pairs together.

Store in an airtight container at room temperature for up to 3 days, or in the refrigerator for up to 7 days.

>>> GLUTEN-FREE—REPLACE THE ALL-PURPOSE FLOUR WITH 1$\frac{1}{4}$ CUPS PLUS 1 TABLESPOON (205 GRAMS) GLUTEN-FREE FLOUR BLEND.

>>> HIGH ALTITUDE—BAKE AT 375°F FOR 5 MINUTES, OR UNTIL THEY LOOK SET AND CRACKED ON TOP.

Some people like frosting so much that they ask for shots of frosting only (which I give them, of course), but I would take a shot of whipped cream over frosting any day. That's what makes these cookies so special to me—they are filled with whipped cream. So light and perfectly sweet! And such a perfect complement to the richness of the brown butter.

Makes 15 sandwiches

DOUGH

Heaping ¹/₃ cup (85 grams) Brown Butter (page 245), at room temperature

¹/₂ cup (113 grams) packed dark brown sugar

¹/₂ teaspoon vanilla extract

2 large eggs

1 large egg yolk

2 cups (255 grams) all-purpose flour

¹/₂ teaspoon baking soda

¹/₂ teaspoon fine sea salt

Cane sugar for topping

FILLING

1 cup (237 milliliters) heavy whipping cream

1¹/₂ teaspoons cane sugar

¹/₂ teaspoon vanilla extract

Preheat the oven to 375°F. Line 2 cookie sheets with parchment paper.

In the bowl of a stand mixer fitted with the paddle attachment, add the brown butter, dark brown sugar, and vanilla extract, and mix on low until combined.

Add the eggs and egg yolk, and mix slightly, just enough to break the yolks.

In a separate bowl, whisk together the flour, baking soda, and sea salt. Add the flour mixture to the butter mixture, and mix on low until combined into a dough.

Using your hands, form the dough into 30 balls, and place them on the prepared cookie sheets about 1 inch apart (15 should fit on each cookie sheet). Flatten them until they are very thin, 2 to 2½ inches in diameter. Once flattened, they can be fairly close together as they won't spread very much while baking.

Bake for 7 minutes, or until set and cracked on top.

Sprinkle with cane sugar immediately after they come out of the oven. Let cool completely on the cookie sheets.

To make the filling: In the bowl of a stand mixer fitted with the whisk attachment, add the cream, cane sugar, and vanilla extract. Whisk on low, then gradually increase the speed to high as the cream thickens. Whip until the cream is thick enough that it doesn't fall off the whisk. Transfer the whipped cream to a piping bag fitted with Ateco tip #864.

Pair the cookies together by size, and turn over every other cookie. Pipe a swirl of whipped cream onto each turned-over cookie, starting near the outer edge and spiraling toward the middle. Sandwich the pairs together.

Store in an airtight container in the refrigerator for up to 7 days.

>>> GLUTEN-FREE—REPLACE THE ALL-PURPOSE FLOUR WITH 1 $^3/_4$ CUPS (269 GRAMS) GLUTEN-FREE FLOUR BLEND.

>>> HIGH ALTITUDE—BAKE AT 375°F FOR 5 MINUTES, OR UNTIL SET AND CRACKED ON TOP.

When I opened Dessert'D, I wanted to become known for being the bakery with new and interesting flavors. That's why I didn't serve chocolate chip cookies at first—I thought they were too traditional. But when customers walked up to the counter and ordered chocolate chip cookies without even looking at all the other awesome cookies we had in the pastry case, I knew we had to give the people what they wanted. As a compromise, I created the Chocolate Chip Sandwich Cookie, and now we serve them daily. It's new and traditional at the same time. Plus, they're so good that even I am guilty of eating them all the time!

Makes 18 sandwiches

DOUGH

1 cup (226 grams) salted butter, softened

1 cup (142 grams) powdered sugar, sifted

1 tablespoon vanilla extract

2 cups (255 grams) all-purpose flour

3/4 cup (142 grams) semisweet chocolate chips

FILLING

1 1/4 cups plus 3 tablespoons (205 grams) powdered sugar, sifted

1/2 cup (113 grams) salted butter, softened

1/4 cup (21 grams) Dutch cocoa powder, sifted

1 to 2 teaspoons milk

Preheat the oven to 350°F. Line 2 cookie sheets with parchment paper.

To make the dough: In the bowl of a stand mixer fitted with the paddle attachment, add the butter, powdered sugar, and vanilla extract. Mix on low just until you no longer see powdered sugar. There should still be chunks of butter; do not overmix.

Add the flour and the chocolate chips, and mix on low until combined into a smooth dough; it should feel like play dough in your hands.

Using your hands, form the dough into 36 balls, and place them on the prepared cookie sheets about 1 inch apart (18 should fit on each cookie sheet). Flatten each ball slightly. They should look like disks that are about 1¾ inches in diameter.

Bake for 13 minutes, or until lightly browned on the bottom. Let cool completely on the cookie sheets.

To make the filling: In the bowl of a stand mixer fitted with the paddle attachment, add the powdered sugar, butter, cocoa, and milk. Mix on low until combined, increase the speed to high, and mix for 1 minute more, or until light and fluffy. Transfer the filling to a piping bag with no tip.

(continues)

Pair the cookies together by size, and turn over every other cookie. Pipe filling onto each turned-over cookie, and sandwich the pairs together.

Store in an airtight container at room temperature for up to 3 days, or in the refrigerator for up to 7 days.

>>> GLUTEN-FREE—REPLACE THE ALL-PURPOSE FLOUR WITH A SCANT 1$\frac{1}{2}$ CUPS (226 GRAMS) GLUTEN-FREE FLOUR BLEND AND $\frac{1}{2}$ CUP PLUS 1 TABLESPOON (57 GRAMS) COCONUT FLOUR.

>>> HIGH ALTITUDE—BAKE AT 350°F FOR 12 MINUTES, OR UNTIL LIGHTLY BROWNED ON THE BOTTOM.

When I first opened the bake shop, I would often name a cookie after one of my friends or relatives. A snickerdoodle covered in cookie glaze was called the Chubby Dougie, after my brother Doug (who is anything but chubby). We quickly realized that the all-over glaze caused the freshly baked cookies to stick together, making a big mess in the pastry case. We decided to turn the glaze into a filling and the regular cookie into a sandwich cookie—no mess, no stress. Bonus: with the new name I no longer have to explain to every customer who Doug is.

Makes 18 sandwiches

DOUGH

1 cup (226 grams) salted butter, softened

1 cup (142 grams) powdered sugar, sifted

1 tablespoon vanilla extract

2 cups (255 grams) all-purpose flour

TOPPING

2 tablespoons cane sugar

1 teaspoon cinnamon

FILLING

1 1/2 cups plus 1 tablespoon (227 grams) powdered sugar, sifted

1/2 cup (113 grams) salted butter, softened

1/2 teaspoon ground vanilla bean

1 to 2 teaspoons milk

Preheat the oven to 350°F. Line 2 cookie sheets with parchment paper.

To make the dough: In the bowl of a stand mixer fitted with the paddle attachment, add the butter, powdered sugar, and vanilla extract. Mix on low until you no longer see powdered sugar. There should still be chunks of butter; do not overmix.

Add the flour, and mix on low until combined into a smooth dough; it should feel like play dough in your hands.

To make the topping: In a small dish mix together the cane sugar and cinnamon, and set aside.

Using your hands, form the dough into 36 balls and place them on the prepared cookie sheets about 1 inch apart (18 should fit on each cookie sheet). Flatten each ball slightly. They should look like disks that are about 1¾ inches in diameter.

Dip the top of each ball of dough into the cinnamon and sugar mixture, and return it to the cookie sheet.

Bake for 13 minutes, or until lightly browned on the bottom. Let cool completely on the cookie sheets.

To make the filling: In the bowl of a stand mixer fitted with the paddle attachment, add the powdered sugar, butter, vanilla bean, and milk. Mix on low until combined, increase the speed to high, and mix for 1 minute more, or until light and fluffy. Transfer the filling to a piping bag with no tip.

(continues)

Pair the cookies together by size, and turn over every other cookie. Pipe filling onto each turned-over cookie, and sandwich the pairs together.

Store in an airtight container at room temperature for up to 3 days, or in the refrigerator for up to 7 days.

>>> GLUTEN-FREE—REPLACE THE ALL-PURPOSE FLOUR WITH A SCANT $1\frac{1}{2}$ CUPS (226 GRAMS) GLUTEN-FREE FLOUR BLEND AND $\frac{1}{2}$ CUP PLUS 1 TABLESPOON (57 GRAMS) COCONUT FLOUR.

>>> HIGH ALTITUDE—BAKE AT 350°F FOR 12 MINUTES, OR UNTIL LIGHTLY BROWNED ON THE BOTTOM.

My mom would usually sit with us while we went through our Halloween candy; we'd tally up the treats we actually liked versus the ones we wanted to trade. Whenever we pulled out a small pack of Nutter Butter cookies (which was surprisingly often), she would snatch it up before anyone else could declare they didn't want it. To this day, I don't know if I liked those cookies or not, because I literally never ate one—Mom stole them all. I created my own version here. Hands off, Mom.

Makes 18 sandwiches

DOUGH

1 cup (226 grams) salted butter, softened

$3/4$ cup plus 1 tablespoon (113 grams) powdered sugar, sifted

1 tablespoon plus 1 teaspoon raw honey

1 tablespoon vanilla extract

2 cups (255 grams) all-purpose flour

$1/2$ teaspoon cinnamon

FILLING

$1 1/2$ cups plus 1 tablespoon (227 grams) powdered sugar, sifted

$1/2$ cup (113 grams) salted butter, softened

2 tablespoons peanut butter

$1/2$ teaspoon vanilla extract

1 to 2 teaspoons milk

Preheat the oven to 350°F. Line 2 cookie sheets with parchment paper.

To make the dough: In the bowl of a stand mixer fitted with the paddle attachment, add the butter, powdered sugar, honey, and vanilla extract. Mix on low just until you no longer see powdered sugar. There should still be chunks of butter; do not overmix.

Add the flour and cinnamon, and mix on low until combined into a smooth dough; it should feel like play dough in your hands.

Using your hands, form the dough into 36 balls, and place them on the prepared cookie sheets about 1 inch apart (18 should fit on each cookie sheet). Flatten each ball slightly. They should look like disks that are about 1¾ inches in diameter.

Bake for 13 minutes, or until lightly browned on the bottom. Let cool completely on the cookie sheets.

To make the filling: In the bowl of a stand mixer fitted with the paddle attachment, add the powdered sugar, butter, peanut butter, vanilla extract, and milk. Mix on low until combined, increase the speed to high, and mix for 1 minute more, or until light and fluffy. Transfer the filling to a piping bag with no tip.

(continues)

Pair the cookies together by size, and turn over every other cookie. Pipe filling onto each turned-over cookie, and sandwich the pairs together.

Store in an airtight container at room temperature for up to 3 days, or in the refrigerator for up to 7 days.

>>> GLUTEN-FREE—REPLACE THE ALL-PURPOSE FLOUR WITH A SCANT $1^{1}/_{2}$ CUPS (226 GRAMS) GLUTEN-FREE FLOUR BLEND AND $^{1}/_{2}$ CUP PLUS 1 TABLESPOON (57 GRAMS) COCONUT FLOUR.

>>> HIGH ALTITUDE—BAKE AT 350°F FOR 12 MINUTES, OR UNTIL LIGHTLY BROWNED ON THE BOTTOM.

If ever two flavors deserved to be together, it's coconut and lemon. What a perfect combination of sweet and tart. Together they make a wonderfully light sandwich cookie— the ideal addition to your next picnic, BBQ, or beach day. I like to use natural colors in my cookies, so I recommend ColorKitchen yellow dye for the perfect pastel hue, or you can leave them uncolored.

Makes 18 sandwiches

DOUGH

1 cup (226 grams) salted butter, softened

1 cup (142 grams) powdered sugar, sifted

1 tablespoon vanilla extract

1 teaspoon coconut extract

2 cups (255 grams) all-purpose flour

1 cup (85 grams) unsweetened finely shredded coconut

FILLING

1½ cups plus 1 tablespoon (227 grams) powdered sugar, sifted

½ cup (113 grams) salted butter, softened

1 teaspoon lemon flavor

¼ teaspoon ColorKitchen yellow dye (optional)

1 teaspoon water (if using food coloring)

Preheat the oven to 350°F. Line 2 cookie sheets with parchment paper.

To make the dough: In the bowl of a stand mixer fitted with the paddle attachment, add the butter, powdered sugar, vanilla extract, and coconut extract. Mix on low just until you no longer see powdered sugar. There should still be chunks of butter; do not overmix.

Add the flour and coconut, and mix on low until combined into a smooth dough; it should feel like play dough in your hands.

Using your hands, form the dough into 36 balls, and place them on the prepared cookie sheets about 1 inch apart (18 should fit on each cookie sheet). Flatten each ball slightly. They should look like disks that are about 1¾ inches in diameter.

Bake for 13 minutes, or until lightly browned on the bottom. Let cool completely on the cookie sheets.

To make the filling: In the bowl of a stand mixer fitted with the paddle attachment, add the powdered sugar, butter, lemon flavor, and the dye and water, if using. Mix on low until combined, increase the speed to high, and mix for 1 minute more, or until light and fluffy. Transfer the filling to a piping bag with no tip.

Pair the cookies together by size, and turn over every other cookie. Pipe filling onto each turned-over cookie, and sandwich the pairs together.

Store in an airtight container at room temperature for up to 3 days, or in the refrigerator for up to 7 days.

>>> GLUTEN-FREE—REPLACE THE ALL-PURPOSE FLOUR WITH A SCANT 1 1/2 CUPS (226 GRAMS) GLUTEN-FREE FLOUR BLEND AND 1/2 CUP PLUS 1 TABLESPOON (57 GRAMS) COCONUT FLOUR.

>>> HIGH ALTITUDE—BAKE AT 350°F FOR 12 MINUTES, OR UNTIL LIGHTLY BROWNED ON THE BOTTOM.

If there's one thing I've learned after owning a bakery, it's this: if it contains salted caramel, people will want it. This sandwich cookie is no exception.

Makes 18 sandwiches

DOUGH

1 cup (226 grams) salted butter, softened

1 cup (142 grams) powdered sugar, sifted

1 tablespoon vanilla extract

1 2/3 cups (212 grams) all-purpose flour

1/2 cup (43 grams) Dutch cocoa powder, sifted

TOPPING

1 teaspoon cane sugar

1 teaspoon fine sea salt

FILLING

1 1/2 cups plus 1 tablespoon (227 grams) powdered sugar, sifted

1/2 cup (113 grams) salted butter, softened

Heaping 1 tablespoon plus 1/3 cup Caramel Sauce (page 253), divided

Preheat the oven to 350°F. Line 2 cookie sheets with parchment paper.

To make the dough: In the bowl of a stand mixer fitted with the paddle attachment, add the butter, powdered sugar, and vanilla extract. Mix on low just until you no longer see powdered sugar. There should still be chunks of butter; do not overmix.

Add the flour and cocoa, and mix on low until combined into a smooth dough; it should feel like play dough in your hands.

Using your hands, form the dough into 36 balls, and place them on the prepared cookie sheets about 1 inch apart (18 should fit on each cookie sheet). Flatten each ball slightly. They should look like disks that are about 1¾ inches in diameter.

Bake for 13 minutes, or until the edges appear mostly dry and set. Let cool completely on the cookie sheets.

To make the topping: In a small dish, mix together the cane sugar and sea salt. Set aside.

To make the filling: In the bowl of a stand mixer fitted with the paddle attachment, add the powdered sugar, butter, and 1 heaping tablespoon caramel sauce. Mix on low until combined; increase the speed to high, and mix for 1 minute more, or until light and fluffy. Transfer the filling to a piping bag with no tip.

Load the remaining 1/3 cup caramel sauce into another piping bag fitted with Ateco tip #56.

Pair the cookies together by size, and turn over every other cookie. Pipe a circle of caramel sauce around the edge

(continues)

of each turned-over cookie, leaving the center for the buttercream filling. Sprinkle some of the topping onto the caramel sauce.

Pipe the buttercream filling onto the center of each caramel-rimmed cookie, and sandwich the pairs together.

Store in an airtight container at room temperature for up to 3 days, or in the refrigerator for up to 7 days.

>>> GLUTEN-FREE—REPLACE THE ALL-PURPOSE FLOUR WITH 1$\frac{1}{3}$ CUPS (212 GRAMS) GLUTEN-FREE FLOUR BLEND AND $\frac{1}{4}$ CUP PLUS 1 TABLESPOON (28 GRAMS) COCONUT FLOUR.

>>> HIGH ALTITUDE—BAKE AT 350°F FOR 12 MINUTES, OR UNTIL THE EDGES APPEAR MOSTLY DRY AND SET.

The thought of sweet graham crackers, gooey marshmallow, and rich chocolate will make pretty much anyone happy. As kids we would roast marshmallows on our stove, until my brother put his finger in the open flame. That stopped our s'more-making real quick. If you have a kitchen torch, you can toast the edges of the marshmallow filling, and the result will almost taste like you made it over an open fire. And it will be a lot safer, too.

Makes 18 sandwiches

DOUGH

8 (127 grams) honey graham crackers

1 cup (226 grams) salted butter, softened

1 cup (142 grams) powdered sugar, sifted

1 tablespoon vanilla extract

1¼ cups (160 grams) all-purpose flour

FILLING

1 tablespoon cold water plus 2 tablespoons room-temperature water, divided

1½ teaspoons gelatin

½ cup (113 grams) cane sugar

¼ cup (78 grams) light corn syrup

⅛ teaspoon fine sea salt

⅛ teaspoon ground vanilla bean

⅓ cup Chocolate Ganache (page 257)

Preheat the oven to 350°F. Line 2 cookie sheets with parchment paper.

To make the dough: Place the graham crackers in the bowl of a food processor, and pulse into a fine powder. Set aside.

In the bowl of a stand mixer fitted with the paddle attachment, add the butter, powdered sugar, and vanilla extract. Mix on low until you no longer see powdered sugar. There should still be chunks of butter; do not overmix.

Add the flour and graham crackers, and mix on low until combined into a smooth dough; it should feel like play dough in your hands.

Using your hands, form the dough into 36 balls and place them on the prepared cookie sheets about 1 inch apart (18 should fit on each cookie sheet). Flatten each ball slightly. They should look like disks that are about 1¾ inches in diameter.

Bake for 13 minutes, or until lightly browned on the bottom. Let cool completely on the cookie sheets.

To make the filling: In the bowl of a stand mixer fitted with the whisk attachment, combine the cold water and gelatin, and stir to dissolve.

In a small pot, combine the cane sugar, corn syrup, room-temperature water, and sea salt. Cook over high heat, stirring to dissolve the sugar. As soon as the mixture starts to bubble and rise in the pot, remove it from the heat; immediately pour it over the gelatin.

Starting at low speed, whisk the sugar-gelatin mixture,

(continues)

slowly increasing the speed to full speed, until the mixture has turned bright white and fluffy. This will take only a few minutes. Add the vanilla bean, and whisk to combine completely. Transfer the filling to a piping bag with no tip.

Pair the cookies together by size, and turn over every other cookie.

Spoon the chocolate ganache into a second piping bag fitted with Ateco tip #56. Pipe a circle of ganache around the edge of each turned-over cookie.

Pipe the marshmallow filling into the center of each turned-over cookie. Sandwich the pairs together.

Torch the marshmallow filling that is exposed around the edges of the cookie sandwich (optional).

Store in an airtight container at room temperature for up to 3 days.

>>> GLUTEN-FREE—USE GLUTEN-FREE GRAHAM CRACKERS; BE SURE TO MEASURE BY WEIGHT AS GLUTEN-FREE GRAHAMS COME IN DIFFERENT SIZES. REPLACE THE ALL-PURPOSE FLOUR WITH $^3/_4$ CUP (117 GRAMS) GLUTEN-FREE FLOUR BLEND AND $^1/_2$ CUP (49 GRAMS) COCONUT FLOUR.

>>> HIGH ALTITUDE—BAKE AT 350°F FOR 12 MINUTES, OR UNTIL LIGHTLY BROWNED ON THE BOTTOM.

The combination of chocolate, vanilla, and strawberry is a classic, usually enjoyed as a popular ice cream. Obviously I had to make it into a cookie.

Makes 18 sandwiches

VANILLA DOUGH

1/2 cup (113 grams) salted butter, softened

1/2 cup (71 grams) powdered sugar, sifted

1 1/2 teaspoons vanilla extract

1 cup (127 grams) all-purpose flour

CHOCOLATE DOUGH

1/2 cup (113 grams) salted butter, softened

1/2 cup (71 grams) powdered sugar, sifted

1 1/2 teaspoons vanilla extract

2/3 cup plus 3 tablespoons (106 grams) all-purpose flour

1/4 cup (21 grams) Dutch cocoa powder, sifted

FILLING

1 cup plus 3 tablespoons (170 grams) powdered sugar, sifted

1/4 cup (57 grams) salted butter, softened

2 tablespoons plus 1/2 cup Strawberry Preserves (page 266), divided

Preheat the oven to 350°F. Line 2 cookie sheets with parchment paper.

Make the vanilla dough first so you don't have to wash the mixing bowl to make the chocolate dough. In the bowl of a stand mixer fitted with the paddle attachment, add the butter, powdered sugar, and vanilla extract. Mix on low just until you no longer see powdered sugar. There should still be chunks of butter; do not overmix.

Add the flour, and mix on low until combined into a smooth dough; it should feel like play dough in your hands.

Using your hands, form the dough into 18 balls and place them on a prepared cookie sheet about 1 inch apart. Flatten each ball slightly. They should look like disks that are about 1¾ inches in diameter.

Bake for 13 minutes, or until lightly browned on the bottom. Let cool completely on the cookie sheets.

To make the chocolate dough: In the same bowl of the stand mixer fitted with the paddle attachment, add the butter, powdered sugar, and vanilla extract. Mix on low just until you no longer see powdered sugar. There should still be chunks of butter; do not overmix.

Add the flour and cocoa, and mix on low until combined into a smooth dough; it should feel like play dough in your hands.

Using your hands, form the dough into 18 balls and place them on a prepared cookie sheet about 1 inch apart. Flatten each ball slightly. They should look like disks that are about 1¾ inches in diameter.

Bake for 13 minutes, or until the edges appear set and mostly dry. Let cool completely on the cookie sheets.

(continues)

To make the filling: In the bowl of a stand mixer fitted with the paddle attachment, add the powdered sugar, butter, and 2 tablespoons strawberry preserves. Mix on low until combined, increase the speed to high, and mix for 1 minute more, or until light and fluffy. Transfer the frosting to a piping bag fitted with Ateco tip #10.

Pair the cookies together by size, one vanilla cookie with one chocolate cookie. Turn over all the vanilla cookies. Pipe a circle of strawberry buttercream filling around the outer edge of each turned-over vanilla cookie. Fill the inside of the circle with strawberry preserves, about 1 teaspoon per cookie. Sandwich with the chocolate cookie.

Store in an airtight container in the refrigerator for up to 7 days.

>>> GLUTEN-FREE—FOR THE VANILLA DOUGH, REPLACE THE ALL-PURPOSE FLOUR WITH A SCANT $3/4$ CUP (113 GRAMS) GLUTEN-FREE FLOUR BLEND AND $1/4$ CUP PLUS 1 TABLESPOON (28 GRAMS) COCONUT FLOUR. FOR THE CHOCOLATE DOUGH, REPLACE THE ALL-PURPOSE FLOUR WITH $1/2$ CUP PLUS 3 TABLESPOONS (106 GRAMS) GLUTEN-FREE FLOUR BLEND AND $2 1/2$ TABLESPOONS (14 GRAMS) COCONUT FLOUR.

>>> HIGH ALTITUDE—BAKE AT 350°F FOR 12 MINUTES, OR UNTIL LIGHTLY BROWNED ON THE BOTTOM.

This recipe reinvents the classic chocolate sandwich cookie with vanilla filling. I use activated charcoal to help give the dough that signature super-black color. And mine have more cream filling than the store-bought variety—just saying.

Makes 24 sandwiches

DOUGH

1 cup (226 grams) salted butter, softened

1 cup (142 grams) powdered sugar, sifted

1 tablespoon vanilla extract

1 2/3 cups (212 grams) all-purpose flour, plus more for rolling

3/4 cup (64 grams) Dutch cocoa powder, sifted

1 tablespoon activated charcoal powder

FILLING

2 cups (283 grams) powdered sugar, sifted

1/2 cup (113 grams) salted butter, softened

2 tablespoons heavy whipping cream

1/2 teaspoon vanilla extract

1/2 teaspoon ground vanilla bean

Preheat the oven to 350°F. Line 2 cookie sheets with parchment paper.

To make the dough: In the bowl of a stand mixer fitted with the paddle attachment, add the butter, powdered sugar, and vanilla extract. Mix on low just until you no longer see powdered sugar. There should still be chunks of butter; do not overmix.

Add the flour, cocoa, and activated charcoal, and mix until a smooth dough forms. It should feel like play dough in your hands.

On a floured work surface, roll out the cookie dough to 1/4 inch thick; use more flour if the dough is sticking. Using a 2½-inch circle cookie cutter, cut out 48 cookies. Place them at least 1 inch apart on the prepared cookie sheets. (You should be able to fit 12 cookies on each cookie sheet. You will need to reuse the cookie sheets to bake all 48 cookies.)

Bake for 13 minutes, or until the edges appear set and mostly dry. Let cool completely on the cookie sheets.

To make the filling: In the bowl of a stand mixer fitted with the paddle attachment, add the powdered sugar, butter, whipping cream, vanilla extract, and vanilla bean. Mix on low until combined, increase the speed to high, and mix for 1 minute more, or until light and fluffy. Transfer the filling to a piping bag with no tip.

Pair the cookies together by size, and turn over every other cookie. Pipe filling onto each turned-over cookie, and sandwich the pairs together.

Store in an airtight container at room temperature for up to 3 days, or in the refrigerator for up to 7 days.

>>> GLUTEN-FREE—REPLACE THE ALL-PURPOSE FLOUR WITH 1$\frac{1}{3}$ CUPS (212 GRAMS) GLUTEN-FREE FLOUR BLEND AND $\frac{1}{4}$ CUP PLUS 1 TABLESPOON (28 GRAMS) COCONUT FLOUR.

>>> HIGH ALTITUDE—BAKE AT 350°F FOR 12 MINUTES, OR UNTIL THE EDGES APPEAR SET AND MOSTLY DRY.

FLORENTINES

THE FLORENTINE IS A THIN, crispy cookie made with just a few simple ingredients: butter, cream, sugar, flour, and nuts. The sugar caramelizes in the oven, creating little holes in the cookie, so they are often called lace cookies. For a finishing touch, the cookies are typically drizzled, dipped, or sandwiched with chocolate.

Some say that the Florentine cookie originated in Florence, hence the name, but there are others who claim it originated in France and was created for the love of Florence. Whatever the true story is, someone was on to something, because these cookies are so good!

We started making Florentines at the bakery because we had an excess of leftover almonds. After we ground the nuts to make the almond flour we use in French macarons, there were always bits and pieces of nut remaining that weren't crushed finely enough. We started saving them (we hate waste) and looking for a way to use them. One summer day while we were on vacation, Delaney tried a Florentine at a local bakery. He loved it and thought that adding Florentines to our menu might offer a way to use up all those excess almonds. After testing many batches, we developed a recipe that used the almonds and also omitted flour, which made our Florentines naturally gluten-free—a huge bonus! The next step was to figure out what flavors to offer, because these cookies were too good to serve just one kind. Our sandwich cookies are so popular that we landed on filling Florentines with buttercream to create a sandwich cookie on crack. And we succeeded.

Over time, we developed several varieties—vanilla bean, almond, dark chocolate-dipped. Soon, we were selling Florentines so fast that we didn't have enough almonds left over from the macarons to keep up with demand. Our almond order more than doubled. Now we have standard flavors that we offer every day, plus a special variety for each holiday, and we're constantly creating new ones.

Tips and Tricks

Almonds

We make our Florentines with blanched slivered almonds. If you can't find blanched almonds, it's easy to blanch them yourself. Bring a pot of water to a boil, and add whole, raw almonds. Use about 3 parts water to 1 part almonds, by volume. Boil for 1 minute. Drain the almonds through a strainer, and run them under cold water to cool them. Spread the almonds on a clean kitchen towel, and pat them dry. Using your fingers, remove the skins by gently squeezing the almonds—the skins will pop right off. Let the almonds cool completely before chopping them into slivers.

Grinding

I use a food processor to grind the almonds, and I recommend setting a timer so you know you are grinding for 30 seconds exactly, which will result in the perfect consistency. It's easy to over- or undergrind.

Cooking

First, it's important to make sure your butter is chilled. That means it should be taken straight from the fridge and added to the pot with the sugar, corn syrup, and cream. When cooking this mixture, it's important to bring it to the exact temperature specified in the recipe. When we first started making Florentines, we would bring the mixture to a boil and continue boiling for about a minute, which is what many recipes specify. However, we found that the cooking time varied depending on the consistency of the butter (hence why it needs to be chilled), or depending on different recipes' interpretation of "boil." The finished Florentines were wildly inconsistent. We figured out the optimal temperature for the mixture and started using a digital thermometer, which helped us perfect the recipe. Digital thermometers are inexpensive and are a great investment.

Resting

After the dough is mixed, it needs to rest for about fifteen minutes. This will give it time to cool off a bit. The dough will still be warm but not so hot that you can't touch it with your hands. Then you roll it into balls, which should be done as soon as you can handle the dough. This is the time when you should preheat your oven, so it's ready as soon as the Florentines are ready.

Shaping

When you roll the Florentine dough into balls, make them really small, about the size of a quarter. They will spread out quite a bit while baking, so be sure to put only eleven balls of dough on an 18 x 13-inch cookie sheet to make sure they don't run into each other. I like to place three balls of dough along each long side of the cookie sheet, and then arrange five more in a zigzag pattern down the middle (see photo on next page).

Also, the dough must come to room temperature before you put the cookie sheet in the oven, or it won't bake right. Let the dough balls sit on the cookie sheets at room temperature until they are no longer hot. Sometimes the balls of dough will start to sink or melt a little on the cookie sheet. As long as you wait until the balls of dough come to room temperature before you put them in the oven, the Florentines will come out just fine. There are fine lines between hot, room temperature, and sitting there for too long, so don't forget about them. It's ideal timing if you shape them as soon as you can handle the dough, and once you're done forming all the balls, they will be ready to go in the oven. If the unbaked cookies sit for too long, you might notice that they are a little thicker and smaller once they come out of the oven.

Baking

When baking Florentines, be sure to avoid overcrowding the oven, which will prevent them from browning evenly. Arrange the trays in the oven so there is at least one rack between two cookie sheets. If your oven only has two racks, then bake the Florentines one cookie sheet at a time, or rotate the cookie sheets partway through the baking process for more even browning. The Florentines are done when they are a beautiful golden-brown. Don't be scared to leave them in the oven a few minutes longer to achieve the right color.

Filling

When assembling Florentines to be filled, be sure to pair up cookies of the same size. Some will be a bit larger than others, so if you pair them just before filling you'll be able to create the best-looking Florentines. Sometimes you'll end up with a couple of odd-sized cookies that don't match up well. Those are your "taster" cookies!

It's really important that the butter be soft when making the filling for Florentines; otherwise the frosting will be stiff, which can break the delicate cookies. Powdered sugar clumps easily, so always sift it before mixing it with the other ingredients. Always make sure to whip the frosting very well before adding liquid, because the more you whip it, the fluffier the frosting. Most of the fillings include milk or water. If I'm using a dye to color the frosting, I always use water because the ColorKitchen dyes we use are water-soluble. If I'm not using a food coloring, then I like to use milk, because milk gives the frosting a little extra flavor. Use whichever you prefer. Just add a little more milk or water if the frosting seems too stiff, starting with 1 teaspoon at a time. At the bakery we always use Ateco tip #864 when filling Florentines—it's kinda my thing. But you can use any decorating tip you like, or you can choose not to use a tip at all. Just pipe it right out of the pastry bag.

Storing

Florentines should be stored in a cool, dry place. If you live in a dry climate, storing Florentines at room temperature in a cookie jar or even out on your counter will be just fine. If you live in a more humid climate, you should store Florentines in an airtight container in the refrigerator, so the humidity doesn't make them soggy.

Behold the original Florentine. This thin, crispy cookie tastes of caramel, toffee, and a pleasing sweetness that can be paired with so many flavors. Master this recipe, and then try all the other varieties in the following pages.

Makes 44

1¼ cups (170 grams) blanched slivered almonds

¼ teaspoon fine sea salt

½ cup plus 2 tablespoons (142 grams) cane sugar

¼ cup (57 grams) salted butter, chilled

2 tablespoons heavy whipping cream

1 tablespoon plus 2 teaspoons light corn syrup

½ teaspoon vanilla extract

Process the almonds in a food processor for exactly 30 seconds. Transfer the ground almonds to a plastic mixing bowl, add the sea salt, and whisk together to combine.

In a medium pot over medium heat, mix together the cane sugar, butter, cream, and corn syrup with a high-heat spatula, and cook until the sugar is dissolved. Continue to cook, stirring occasionally, until the mixture reaches 197°F to 200°F on a digital thermometer. Immediately remove from the heat. Pour the hot sugar mixture over the almonds, and stir several times. Add the vanilla extract, and stir to combine completely.

Let the mixture rest at room temperature for about 15 minutes, until it has cooled enough to touch.

Preheat the oven to 350°F. Line 4 cookie sheets with parchment paper.

Using your hands, form the dough into 44 balls and place them on the prepared cookie sheets (11 should fit on each cookie sheet): line up 3 balls of dough along each long side of the cookie sheet, then zigzag 5 additional balls of dough down the middle (see "Shaping," page 167).

Bake for 11 minutes, or until golden-brown. Let cool completely on the cookie sheets.

Store in an airtight container at room temperature for up to 7 days.

>>> HIGH ALTITUDE—BAKE AT 350°F FOR 10 MINUTES, OR UNTIL GOLDEN-BROWN.

DARK CHOCOLATE—DIPPED FLORENTINES

Dipping anything in chocolate just makes it better. And sometimes simple dark chocolate is all you need. These are beautiful and elegant. Wrap some in a box with a pretty ribbon, and you'll have a very nice hostess gift.

Makes 44

1¼ cups (170 grams) blanched slivered almonds

¼ teaspoon sea salt, plus more for sprinkling (optional)

½ cup plus 2 tablespoons (142 grams) cane sugar

¼ cup (57 grams) salted butter, chilled

2 tablespoons heavy whipping cream

1 tablespoon plus 2 teaspoons light corn syrup

½ teaspoon vanilla extract

2 cups (283 grams) finely chopped dark chocolate

>>> HIGH ALTITUDE—BAKE AT 350°F FOR 10 MINUTES, OR UNTIL GOLDEN-BROWN.

Process the almonds in a food processor for exactly 30 seconds. Transfer the ground almonds to a plastic mixing bowl, add ¼ teaspoon sea salt, and whisk together to combine.

In a medium pot over medium heat, mix together the cane sugar, butter, cream, and corn syrup with a high-heat spatula, and cook until the sugar is dissolved. Continue to cook, stirring occasionally, until the mixture reaches 197°F to 200°F on a digital thermometer. Immediately remove from the heat. Pour the hot sugar mixture over the almonds, and stir several times. Add the vanilla extract, and stir to combine completely.

Let the mixture rest at room temperature for about 15 minutes, until it has cooled enough to touch.

Preheat the oven to 350°F. Line 4 cookie sheets with parchment paper.

Using your hands, form the dough into 44 balls and place them on the prepared cookie sheets (11 should fit on each cookie sheet): line up 3 balls of dough along each long side of the cookie sheet, then zigzag 5 additional balls of dough down the middle (see "Shaping," page 167).

Bake for 11 minutes, or until golden-brown. Let cool completely on the cookie sheets.

Temper the dark chocolate using the technique on page 268.

Dip each Florentine halfway into the dark chocolate, and return it to the cookie sheet. Refrigerate for 1 hour to set the chocolate. Sprinkle with sea salt, if using.

Store in an airtight container at room temperature for up to 7 days.

Simple, pure, and perfect. Two crispy Florentines surrounding a creamy milk chocolate filling—it doesn't get much better than this.

Makes 22 sandwiches

1¼ cups (170 grams) blanched slivered almonds

¼ teaspoon fine sea salt

½ cup plus 2 tablespoons (142 grams) cane sugar

¼ cup (57 grams) salted butter, chilled

2 tablespoons heavy whipping cream

1 tablespoon plus 2 teaspoons light corn syrup

½ teaspoon vanilla extract

1 cup plus 3 tablespoons (170 grams) finely chopped milk chocolate

>>> HIGH ALTITUDE—BAKE AT 350°F FOR 10 MINUTES, OR UNTIL GOLDEN-BROWN.

Process the almonds in a food processor for exactly 30 seconds. Transfer the ground almonds to a plastic mixing bowl, add the sea salt, and whisk together to combine.

In a medium pot over medium heat, mix together the cane sugar, butter, cream, and corn syrup with a high-heat spatula, and cook until the sugar is dissolved. Continue to cook, stirring occasionally, until the mixture reaches 197°F to 200°F on a digital thermometer. Immediately remove from the heat. Pour the hot sugar mixture over the almonds, and stir several times. Add the vanilla extract, and stir to combine completely.

Let the mixture rest at room temperature for about 15 minutes, until it has cooled enough to touch.

Preheat the oven to 350°F. Line 4 cookie sheets with parchment paper.

Using your hands, form the dough into 44 balls and place them on the prepared cookie sheets (11 should fit on each cookie sheet): line up 3 balls of dough along each long side of the cookie sheet, then zigzag 5 additional balls of dough down the middle (see "Shaping," page 167).

Bake for 11 minutes, or until golden-brown. Let cool completely on the cookie sheets.

To make the filling: In a double boiler over medium heat, melt the milk chocolate. (No need to temper the chocolate because it will be sandwiched between two Florentines.)

Pair the cookies together by size, and turn over every other one. Using a small spatula, spread chocolate onto each turned-over cookie, sandwich the pairs, and return them to the cookie sheet. Refrigerate for 1 hour to set the chocolate.

Store in an airtight container at room temperature for up to 7 days.

These were the first flavor of Florentine we made for the bakery, and rightfully so. There is something so pure and simple about vanilla, and using ground vanilla beans in the frosting really gives these cookies a true vanilla flavor, one that you can't beat.

Makes 22 sandwiches

DOUGH

1¼ cups (170 grams) blanched slivered almonds

¼ teaspoon fine sea salt

½ cup plus 2 tablespoons (142 grams) cane sugar

¼ cup (57 grams) salted butter, chilled

2 tablespoons heavy whipping cream

1 tablespoon plus 2 teaspoons light corn syrup

½ teaspoon vanilla extract

FILLING

Heaping 2⅓ cups (340 grams) powdered sugar, sifted

¾ cup (170 grams) salted butter, softened

2 teaspoons milk

½ teaspoon ground vanilla bean

To make the dough: Process the almonds in a food processor for exactly 30 seconds. Transfer the ground almonds to a plastic mixing bowl, add the sea salt, and whisk together to combine.

In a medium pot over medium heat, mix together the cane sugar, butter, cream, and corn syrup with a high-heat spatula, and cook until the sugar is dissolved. Continue to cook, stirring occasionally, until the mixture reaches 197°F to 200°F on a digital thermometer. Immediately remove from the heat. Pour the hot sugar mixture over the almonds, and stir several times. Add the vanilla extract, and stir to combine completely.

Let the mixture rest at room temperature for about 15 minutes, until it has cooled enough to touch.

Preheat the oven to 350°F. Line 4 cookie sheets with parchment paper.

Using your hands, form the dough into 44 balls and place them on the prepared cookie sheets (11 should fit on each cookie sheet): line up 3 balls of dough along each long side of the cookie sheet, then zigzag 5 additional balls of dough down the middle (see "Shaping," page 167).

Bake for 11 minutes, or until golden-brown. Let cool completely on the cookie sheets.

To make the filling: In the bowl of a stand mixer fitted with the paddle attachment, add the powdered sugar, butter, milk, and vanilla bean. Mix on low until combined, increase the speed to high, and mix for 1 minute more, or until light and fluffy. Transfer the filling to a piping bag fitted with Ateco tip #864.

Pair the cookies together by size, and turn over every

other one. Pipe a swirl of frosting onto each turned-over cookie, starting at the outer edge and spiraling into the middle. Carefully sandwich the pairs.

Store in an airtight container at room temperature for up to 3 days, or in the refrigerator for up to 7 days.

>>> HIGH ALTITUDE—BAKE AT 350°F FOR 10 MINUTES, OR UNTIL GOLDEN-BROWN.

Almonds on top of almonds. For those who love marzipan, this is the flavor for you. Rather than being overwhelming, the almonds complement each other, and the sweetness paired with the crunch of the Florentine is a lovely combination.

Makes 22 sandwiches

DOUGH

1¼ cups (170 grams) blanched slivered almonds

¼ teaspoon fine sea salt

½ cup plus 2 tablespoons (142 grams) cane sugar

¼ cup (57 grams) salted butter, chilled

2 tablespoons heavy whipping cream

1 tablespoon plus 2 teaspoons light corn syrup

½ teaspoon vanilla extract

FILLING

Heaping 2⅓ cups (340 grams) powdered sugar, sifted

¾ cup (170 grams) salted butter, softened

2 teaspoons almond flavor

1 to 2 teaspoons milk

To make the dough: Process the almonds in a food processor for exactly 30 seconds. Transfer the ground almonds to a plastic mixing bowl, add the sea salt, and whisk together to combine.

In a medium pot over medium heat, mix together the cane sugar, butter, cream, and corn syrup with a high-heat spatula, and cook until the sugar is dissolved. Continue to cook, stirring occasionally, until the mixture reaches 197°F to 200°F on a digital thermometer. Immediately remove from the heat. Pour the hot sugar mixture over the almonds, and stir several times. Add the vanilla extract, and stir to combine completely.

Let the mixture rest at room temperature for about 15 minutes, until it has cooled enough to touch.

Preheat the oven to 350°F. Line 4 cookie sheets with parchment paper.

Using your hands, form the dough into 44 balls and place them on the prepared cookie sheets (11 should fit on each cookie sheet): line up 3 balls of dough along each long side of the cookie sheet, then zigzag 5 additional balls of dough down the middle (see "Shaping," page 167).

Bake for 11 minutes, or until golden-brown. Let cool completely on the cookie sheets.

To make the filling: In the bowl of a stand mixer fitted with the paddle attachment, add the powdered sugar, butter, almond flavor, and milk. Mix on low until combined, increase the speed to high, and mix for 1 minute more, or until light and fluffy. Transfer the filling to a piping bag fitted with Ateco tip #864.

Pair the cookies together by size, and turn over every other one. Pipe a swirl of frosting onto each turned-over cookie, starting around the outer edge and spiraling into the middle. Carefully sandwich the pairs.

Store in an airtight container at room temperature for up to 3 days, or in the refrigerator for up to 7 days.

>>> HIGH ALTITUDE—BAKE AT 350°F FOR 10 MINUTES, OR UNTIL GOLDEN-BROWN.

BUTTERSCOTCH FLORENTINES

Whenever I ate butterscotch candy as a kid, I was usually sneaking it. My grandparents were the only ones who ever had them in the house, and my Grandma Booda was even stricter about sweets than my mom (at least I knew where Mom got it from). So anything butterscotch takes me back to being a five-year-old kid, removing that gold candy wrapper, my heart beating fast because I didn't want to get caught while anticipating the salty sweetness I was about to consume. I will forever love butterscotch because it always makes me feel like a rebel.

Makes 22 sandwiches

DOUGH

1¼ cups (170 grams) blanched slivered almonds

¼ teaspoon fine sea salt

½ cup plus 2 tablespoons (142 grams) cane sugar

¼ cup (57 grams) salted butter, chilled

2 tablespoons heavy whipping cream

1 tablespoon plus 2 teaspoons light corn syrup

½ teaspoon vanilla extract

FILLING

Heaping 2⅓ cups (340 grams) powdered sugar, sifted

¾ cup (170 grams) salted butter, softened

3 tablespoons Butterscotch Sauce (page 249)

To make the dough: Process the almonds in a food processor for exactly 30 seconds. Transfer the ground almonds to a plastic mixing bowl, add the sea salt, and whisk together to combine.

In a medium pot over medium heat, mix together the cane sugar, butter, cream, and corn syrup with a high-heat spatula, and cook until the sugar is dissolved. Continue to cook, stirring occasionally, until the mixture reaches 197°F to 200°F on a digital thermometer. Immediately remove from the heat. Pour the hot sugar mixture over the almonds, and stir several times. Add the vanilla extract, and stir to combine completely.

Let the mixture rest at room temperature for about 15 minutes, until it has cooled enough to touch.

Preheat the oven to 350°F. Line 4 cookie sheets with parchment paper.

Using your hands, form the dough into 44 balls and place them on the prepared cookie sheets (11 should fit on each cookie sheet): line up 3 balls of dough along each long side of the cookie sheet, then zigzag 5 additional balls of dough down the middle (see "Shaping," page 167).

Bake for 11 minutes, or until golden-brown. Let cool completely on the cookie sheets.

To make the filling: In the bowl of a stand mixer fitted with the paddle attachment, add the powdered sugar, butter, and

(continues)

butterscotch sauce. Mix on low until combined, increase the speed to high, and mix for 1 minute more, or until light and fluffy. Transfer the filling to a piping bag fitted with Ateco tip #864.

Pair the cookies together by size, and turn over every other one. Pipe a swirl of frosting onto each turned-over cookie, starting around the outer edge and spiraling into the middle. Carefully sandwich the pairs.

Store in an airtight container at room temperature for up to 3 days, or in the refrigerator for up to 7 days.

>>> HIGH ALTITUDE—BAKE AT 350°F FOR 10 MINUTES, OR UNTIL GOLDEN-BROWN.

All the major happenings in my life have been celebrated with cookies. Sometimes you just need something sweet that will put a smile on your face, and for me that's a cookie. With their lacey cookie and colorful filling, these Florentines are fitting when you want to make a big deal out of any event.

Makes 22 sandwiches

DOUGH

1 1/4 cups (170 grams) blanched slivered almonds

1/4 teaspoon fine sea salt

1/2 cup plus 2 tablespoons (142 grams) cane sugar

1/4 cup (57 grams) salted butter, chilled

2 tablespoons heavy whipping cream

1 tablespoon plus 2 teaspoons light corn syrup

1/2 teaspoon vanilla extract

FILLING

Heaping 2 1/3 cups (340 grams) powdered sugar, sifted

3/4 cup (170 grams) salted butter, softened

1 to 2 teaspoons milk

1 teaspoon vanilla extract

1/2 cup (85 grams) rainbow sprinkles

To make the dough: Process the almonds in a food processor for exactly 30 seconds. Transfer the ground almonds to a plastic mixing bowl, add the sea salt, and whisk together to combine.

In a medium pot over medium heat, mix together the cane sugar, butter, cream, and corn syrup with a high-heat spatula, and cook until the sugar is dissolved. Continue to cook, stirring occasionally, until the mixture reaches 197°F to 200°F on a digital thermometer. Immediately remove from the heat. Pour the hot sugar mixture over the almonds, and stir several times. Add the vanilla extract, and stir to combine completely.

Let the mixture rest at room temperature for about 15 minutes, until it has cooled enough to touch.

Preheat the oven to 350°F. Line 4 cookie sheets with parchment paper.

Using your hands, form the dough into 44 balls and place them on the prepared cookie sheets (11 should fit on each cookie sheet): line up 3 balls of dough along each long side of the cookie sheet, then zigzag 5 additional balls of dough down the middle (see "Shaping," page 167).

Bake for 11 minutes, or until golden-brown. Let cool completely on the cookie sheets.

To make the filling: In the bowl of a stand mixer fitted with the paddle attachment, add the powdered sugar, butter, milk, and vanilla extract. Mix on low until combined, increase the speed to high, and mix for 1 minute more, or

(continues)

until light and fluffy. Add the rainbow sprinkles, and mix to combine. Transfer the filling to a piping bag with no tip (the sprinkles won't come out very well through decorative tips).

Pair the cookies together by size, and turn over every other one. Pipe a dollop of frosting onto each turned-over cookie. Carefully sandwich the pairs.

Store in an airtight container at room temperature for up to 3 days, or in the refrigerator for up to 7 days.

>>> HIGH ALTITUDE—BAKE AT 350°F FOR 10 MINUTES, OR UNTIL GOLDEN-BROWN.

SNICKERDOODLE FLORENTINES

I love the cinnamon-sugar combination that defines the snickerdoodle, so I had to create a Florentine with the same flavors. These are so delicious you may never eat a regular snickerdoodle again.

Makes 22 sandwiches

DOUGH

1¼ cups (170 grams) blanched slivered almonds

¼ teaspoon fine sea salt

½ cup plus 2 tablespoons (142 grams) cane sugar

¼ cup (57 grams) salted butter, chilled

2 tablespoons heavy whipping cream

1 tablespoon plus 2 teaspoons light corn syrup

½ teaspoon vanilla extract

FILLING

Heaping 2⅓ cups (340 grams) powdered sugar, sifted

¾ cup (170 grams) salted butter, softened

1 to 2 teaspoons milk

1 teaspoon cinnamon

½ teaspoon ground vanilla bean

To make the dough: Process the almonds in a food processor for exactly 30 seconds. Transfer the ground almonds to a plastic mixing bowl, add the sea salt, and whisk together to combine.

In a medium pot over medium heat, mix together the cane sugar, butter, cream, and corn syrup with a high-heat spatula, and cook until the sugar is dissolved. Continue to cook, stirring occasionally, until the mixture reaches 197°F to 200°F on a digital thermometer. Immediately remove from the heat. Pour the hot sugar mixture over the almonds, and stir several times. Add the vanilla extract, and stir to combine completely.

Let the mixture rest at room temperature for about 15 minutes, until it has cooled enough to touch.

Preheat the oven to 350°F. Line 4 cookie sheets with parchment paper.

Using your hands, form the dough into 44 balls and place them on the prepared cookie sheets (11 should fit on each cookie sheet): line up 3 balls of dough along each long side of the cookie sheet, then zigzag 5 additional balls of dough down the middle (see "Shaping," page 167).

Bake for 11 minutes, or until golden-brown. Let cool completely on the cookie sheets.

To make the filling: In the bowl of a stand mixer fitted with the paddle attachment, add the powdered sugar, butter, milk, cinnamon, and vanilla bean. Mix on low until combined, increase the speed to high, and mix for 1 minute more, or until light and fluffy. Transfer the filling to a piping bag fitted with Ateco tip #864.

Pair the cookies together by size, and turn over every other one. Pipe a swirl of frosting onto each turned-over cookie, starting around the outer edge and spiraling into the middle. Carefully sandwich the pairs together.

Store in an airtight container at room temperature for up to 3 days, or in the refrigerator for up to 7 days.

>>> HIGH ALTITUDE—BAKE AT 350°F FOR 10 MINUTES, OR UNTIL GOLDEN-BROWN.

The spices used in this recipe will transport you straight to Christmas, even if it's July. It doesn't have to be the holidays to feel warm and fuzzy inside—make these any time of year.

Makes 22 sandwiches

DOUGH

1 1/4 cups (170 grams) blanched slivered almonds

1/4 teaspoon fine sea salt

1/2 cup plus 2 tablespoons (142 grams) cane sugar

1/4 cup (57 grams) salted butter, chilled

2 tablespoons heavy whipping cream

1 tablespoon plus 2 teaspoons light corn syrup

1/2 teaspoon vanilla extract

FILLING

Heaping 2 1/3 cups (340 grams) powdered sugar, sifted

3/4 cup (170 grams) salted butter, softened

2 teaspoons milk

1 teaspoon cinnamon

1 teaspoon ginger

1 teaspoon cloves

To make the dough: Process the almonds in a food processor for exactly 30 seconds. Transfer the ground almonds to a plastic mixing bowl, add the sea salt, and whisk together to combine.

In a medium pot over medium heat, mix together the cane sugar, butter, cream, and corn syrup with a high-heat spatula, and cook until the sugar is dissolved. Continue to cook, stirring occasionally, until the mixture reaches 197°F to 200°F on a digital thermometer. Immediately remove from the heat. Pour the hot sugar mixture over the almonds, and stir several times. Add the vanilla extract, and stir to combine completely.

Let the mixture rest at room temperature for about 15 minutes, until it has cooled enough to touch.

Preheat the oven to 350°F. Line 4 cookie sheets with parchment paper.

Using your hands, form the dough into 44 balls and place them on the prepared cookie sheets (11 should fit on each cookie sheet): line up 3 balls of dough along each long side of the cookie sheet, then zigzag 5 additional balls of dough down the middle (see "Shaping," page 167).

Bake for 11 minutes, or until golden-brown. Let cool completely on the cookie sheets.

To make the filling: In the bowl of a stand mixer fitted with the paddle attachment, add the powdered sugar, butter, milk, cinnamon, ginger, and cloves. Mix on low until combined, increase the speed to high, and mix for 1 minute more, or until light and fluffy. Transfer the filling to a piping bag fitted with Ateco tip #864.

(continues)

Pair the cookies together by size, and turn over every other one. Pipe a swirl of frosting onto each turned-over cookie, starting around the outer edge and spiraling into the middle. Carefully sandwich the pairs.

Store in an airtight container at room temperature for up to 3 days, or in the refrigerator for up to 7 days.

>>> HIGH ALTITUDE—BAKE AT 350°F FOR 10 MINUTES, OR UNTIL GOLDEN-BROWN.

The caramel, nutty, and sweet flavor of a Florentine pairs really nicely with banana. It's fun to add color to these; you can easily brighten them up with a little natural yellow dye.

Makes 22 sandwiches

DOUGH

1¼ cups (170 grams) blanched slivered almonds

¼ teaspoon fine sea salt

½ cup plus 2 tablespoons (142 grams) cane sugar

¼ cup (57 grams) salted butter, chilled

2 tablespoons heavy whipping cream

1 tablespoon plus 2 teaspoons light corn syrup

½ teaspoon vanilla extract

FILLING

Heaping 2⅓ cups (340 grams) powdered sugar, sifted

¾ cup (170 grams) salted butter, softened

2 teaspoons banana flavor

¼ teaspoon ColorKitchen yellow dye (optional)

1 teaspoon water

To make the dough: Process the almonds in a food processor for exactly 30 seconds. Transfer the ground almonds to a plastic mixing bowl, add the sea salt, and whisk together to combine.

In a medium pot over medium heat, mix together the cane sugar, butter, cream, and corn syrup with a high-heat spatula, and cook until the sugar is dissolved. Continue to cook, stirring occasionally, until the mixture reaches 197°F to 200°F on a digital thermometer. Immediately remove from the heat. Pour the hot sugar mixture over the almonds, and stir several times. Add the vanilla extract, and stir to combine completely.

Let the mixture rest at room temperature for about 15 minutes, until it has cooled enough to touch.

Preheat the oven to 350°F. Line 4 cookie sheets with parchment paper.

Using your hands, form the dough into 44 balls and place them on the prepared cookie sheets (11 should fit on each cookie sheet): line up 3 balls of dough along each long side of the cookie sheet, then zigzag 5 additional balls of dough down the middle (see "Shaping," page 167).

Bake for 11 minutes, or until golden-brown. Let cool completely on the cookie sheets.

To make the filling: In the bowl of a stand mixer fitted with the paddle attachment, add the powdered sugar, butter, banana flavor, and the yellow dye and water, if using. Mix on low until combined, increase the speed to high, and mix for 1 minute more, or until light and fluffy. Transfer the filling to a piping bag fitted with Ateco tip #864.

(continues)

Pair the cookies together by size, and turn over every other one. Pipe a swirl of frosting onto each turned-over cookie, starting around the outer edge and spiraling into the middle. Carefully sandwich the pairs.

Store in an airtight container at room temperature for up to 3 days, or in the refrigerator for up to 7 days.

>>> HIGH ALTITUDE—BAKE AT 350°F FOR 10 MINUTES, OR UNTIL GOLDEN-BROWN.

I played a lot of team sports growing up, and part of what I loved about them was snack time. A different mom was assigned to bring snacks to each game. My mom always brought healthy snacks. So I lived for whatever the other moms brought, and one of my favorites was what everyone called puppy chow. Basically, it's peanut butter and chocolate melted together, poured over some kind of crunchy cereal, and drenched in powdered sugar. That is exactly what I have done to this Florentine…and I didn't even have to kick a soccer ball—SCORE!

Makes 22 sandwiches

DOUGH

1¼ cups (170 grams) blanched slivered almonds

¼ teaspoon fine sea salt

½ cup plus 2 tablespoons (142 grams) cane sugar

¼ cup (57 grams) salted butter, chilled

2 tablespoons heavy whipping cream

1 tablespoon plus 2 teaspoons light corn syrup

½ teaspoon vanilla extract

FILLING

2 cups plus 3 tablespoons (310 grams) powdered sugar, sifted

¾ cup (170 grams) salted butter, softened

⅓ cup (28 grams) Dutch cocoa powder, sifted

1 tablespoon milk

TOPPING

1 cup plus 3 tablespoons (170 grams) finely chopped milk chocolate

Heaping ¼ cup (85 grams) peanut butter

Powdered sugar for dusting

To make the dough: Process the almonds in a food processor for exactly 30 seconds. Transfer the ground almonds to a plastic mixing bowl, add the sea salt, and whisk together to combine.

In a medium pot over medium heat, mix together the cane sugar, butter, cream, and corn syrup with a high-heat spatula, and cook until dissolved. Continue to cook, stirring occasionally, until the mixture reaches 197°F to 200°F on a digital thermometer. Immediately remove from the heat. Pour the hot sugar mixture over the almonds, and stir several times. Add the vanilla extract, and stir to combine completely.

Let the mixture rest at room temperature for about 15 minutes, until it has cooled enough to touch.

Preheat the oven to 350°F. Line 4 cookie sheets with parchment paper.

Using your hands, form the dough into 44 balls and place them on the prepared cookie sheets (11 should fit on each cookie sheet): line up 3 balls of dough along each long side

(continues)

of the cookie sheet, then zigzag 5 additional balls of dough down the middle (see "Shaping," page 167).

Bake for 11 minutes, or until golden-brown. Let cool completely on the cookie sheets.

To make the filling: In the bowl of a stand mixer fitted with the paddle attachment, add the powdered sugar, butter, cocoa, and milk. Mix on low until combined, increase the speed to high, and mix for 1 minute more, or until light and fluffy. Transfer the filling to a piping bag fitted with Ateco tip #864.

Pair the cookies together by size, and turn over every other one. Pipe a swirl of frosting onto each turned-over cookie, starting around the outer edge and spiraling into the middle. Carefully sandwich the pairs.

To make the topping: Temper the milk chocolate using the technique on page 268. Add the peanut butter, and stir to combine.

Dip each Florentine sandwich halfway into the chocolate mixture, and return it to the cookie sheet. Refrigerate for 1 hour to set the chocolate.

Sift powdered sugar over the top of the cookies.

Store in an airtight container at room temperature for up to 3 days, or in the refrigerator for up to 7 days.

>>> HIGH ALTITUDE—BAKE AT 350°F FOR 10 MINUTES, OR UNTIL GOLDEN-BROWN.

I have never been someone who eats raw cookie dough—shocking, I know! It's probably a good thing, because I own a cookie-baking business and if I ate all the dough, I'd never have any cookies to sell. Part of owning a bakery is baking things for other people, and that is one of the things I love about it. I love making others happy with something as simple as a cookie. My good friend and partner, Kimmy, loves cookie dough–flavored ANYTHING! So these are for her (and for you).

Makes 22 sandwiches

DOUGH

1¼ cups (170 grams) blanched slivered almonds

¼ teaspoon fine sea salt

½ cup plus 2 tablespoons (142 grams) cane sugar

¼ cup (57 grams) salted butter, chilled

2 tablespoons heavy whipping cream

1 tablespoon plus 2 teaspoons light corn syrup

½ teaspoon vanilla extract

FILLING

3 cups plus 3 tablespoons (454 grams) powdered sugar, sifted

1 cup (226 grams) salted butter, softened

¼ cup (57 grams) cane sugar

¼ cup (57 grams) packed dark brown sugar

2 teaspoons vanilla extract

2 teaspoons milk

To make the dough: Process the almonds in a food processor for exactly 30 seconds. Transfer the ground almonds to a plastic mixing bowl, add the sea salt, and whisk together to combine.

In a medium pot over medium heat, mix together the cane sugar, butter, cream, and corn syrup with a high-heat spatula, and cook until the sugar is dissolved. Continue to cook, stirring occasionally, until the mixture reaches 197°F to 200°F on a digital thermometer. Immediately remove from the heat. Pour the hot sugar mixture over the almonds, and stir several times. Add the vanilla extract, and stir to combine completely.

Let the mixture rest at room temperature for about 15 minutes, until it has cooled enough to touch.

Preheat the oven to 350°F. Line 4 cookie sheets with parchment paper.

Using your hands, form the dough into 44 balls and place them on the prepared cookie sheets (11 should fit on each cookie sheet): line up 3 balls of dough along each long side of the cookie sheet, then zigzag 5 additional balls of dough down the middle (see "Shaping," page 167).

Bake for 11 minutes, or until golden-brown. Let cool completely on the cookie sheets.

To make the filling: In the bowl of a stand mixer fitted with the paddle attachment, add the powdered sugar, butter, cane sugar, dark brown sugar, vanilla extract, and milk. Mix

Heaping 1¼ cups (198 grams) finely chopped milk chocolate

on low until combined, increase the speed to high, and mix for 1 minute more, or until light and fluffy. Transfer the filling to a piping bag with no tip.

Pair the cookies together by size, and turn over every other one. Pipe a dollop of frosting onto each turned-over cookie. Carefully sandwich the pairs.

To make the topping: Temper the milk chocolate using the technique on page 268.

Dip each Florentine sandwich halfway into the milk chocolate, and return it to the cookie sheet. Refrigerate for 1 hour to set the chocolate.

Store in an airtight container at room temperature for up to 3 days, or in the refrigerator for up to 7 days.

>>> HIGH ALTITUDE—BAKE AT 350°F FOR 10 MINUTES, OR UNTIL GOLDEN-BROWN.

FRENCH MACARONS

THE COOKIE PART OF THE MACARON ORIGINATED IN ITALY and was
served without a filling. It wasn't until years later that a French chef decided
to fill them with chocolate ganache and sandwich them together, which is
when they became known as French macarons. Today, most macarons are
made with the same ingredients—egg whites, sugar, and almond flour—and
filled with things like buttercream, ganache, jam, and more.

When French macarons are fresh, there is nothing like them in the
world—absolutely nothing! They are a petite, magical little cookie that is
simultaneously light, crispy, chewy, and melts in your mouth.

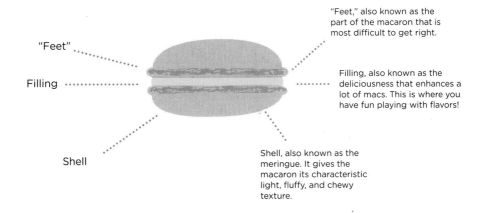

"Feet," also known as the
part of the macaron that is
most difficult to get right.

"Feet"

Filling

Filling, also known as the
deliciousness that enhances a
lot of macs. This is where you
have fun playing with flavors!

Shell

Shell, also known as the
meringue. It gives the
macaron its characteristic
light, fluffy, and chewy
texture.

Tips and Tricks

Almond Flour

You can't have a macaron without almonds. You can use blanched almonds and grind them yourself to create almond flour, or you can buy almond flour already ground. When I first started making macarons, I ground the almonds myself. But as our demand for macarons grew and grew, it became much more efficient to buy almond flour. If you decide to grind your own almonds, use a food processor, and make sure to grind them as fine as you can. But be careful not to grind them too much, because they can turn into almond butter.

Meringue

Macarons are temperamental, so I believe it's important to weigh the ingredients to ensure that the cookies come out properly. Eggs come in different sizes, so it's very important to weigh the eggs. You can always use the excess for breakfast!

I make meringue for macarons a little differently than is called for in other macaron recipes. Instead of gradually adding the sugar while beating the egg whites, my recipe calls for placing the egg whites, sugar, and vanilla extract in the bowl before even turning on the mixer, which is simpler. I use organic cane sugar, which has larger crystals than white granulated sugar, so the mixture needs to be whisked longer for the sugar to be fully incorporated and to dissolve completely. The resulting meringue will look bright white and glossy, and will form stiff peaks.

Sifting

I sift the almond flour and the powdered sugar together. If you're using cocoa powder for chocolate macarons, or a powdered dye for brightly colored macarons, those should be sifted as well. I measure them all directly into the sifter and then sift over the mixing bowl when the meringue is ready. No need to dirty another bowl.

Mixing

After the dry ingredients have been sifted into the meringue, return the whisk and bowl to the mixer, turn the mixer on low, and mix for ten to fifteen rotations, until the dry ingredients start to blend into the meringue (see first photo below). Increase the speed to medium-high, and pulse four to five times to incorporate the batter a little more (see second photo below). At this point the mixture should look about three-quarters combined; you'll still see spots of dry ingredients and parts of meringue. Remove the whisk and mixing bowl from the mixer.

Stirring

Using a spatula, gently fold in the remaining dry ingredients to incorporate them completely. You should only have to fold about five to six times for the batter to be completely combined. At this stage the batter should look like a thick pancake batter. It should not run off the spatula easily.

Piping

Line two cookie sheets with parchment paper. Attach Ateco tip #804 to a piping bag. Place the piping bag in a tall glass or milkshake cup, and fold the edges of the bag down over the edges of the glass. This will make it easy to pour in the batter. Fill the piping bag with batter. Pipe the batter onto the cookie sheets in rounds that are about 1 to 1½ inches in diameter—six across and five down, for a total of thirty per sheet. A trick to help you pipe perfectly sized macarons is to count to two each time you pipe a macaron.

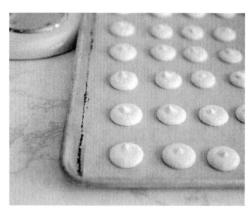

Before banging.

Banging

Banging the cookie sheet on the counter is a classic macaron-making step. It removes air bubbles and smooths out the top of the batter. The banging also helps create the iconic "feet" that are a feature of well-baked macarons. If your macarons don't have feet, that usually means you overstirred the batter. Bang the tray on a solid, flat surface like your kitchen counter several times, turn the cookie sheet around, and bang it several times more. You'll notice that the tops are smoother after this step.

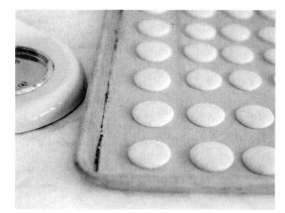

After banging.

Resting

Once the macarons are piped onto the cookie sheets, they should rest for at least forty-five minutes, until a shell or skin develops on the batter. You'll know that the shell has formed when you lightly touch the batter with your finger—it will be smooth and dry. The resting time may vary depending on your climate. If you are in a dry climate it will take less time. A humid climate will take longer. If it's raining or snowing it will take longer. Set a timer for forty-five minutes, check the batter, and if it's not ready, continue to let it rest, checking every ten minutes until the shell or skin forms. But don't let them rest too long, or you'll end up with what I call "clamshell" macarons: one side of the dough rises, and the other side sticks to the foot so it looks like an open clam shell.

Baking

Bake as directed in the recipe. However, if you notice that the feet are starting to flatten out rather than remaining under the macarons, as they should, try this little trick: Open the oven door a couple of times during the baking process. Just open it, and close it right afterward. Sometimes I'll open it after two minutes, then again after another two minutes. This helps dry out the oven, because macarons do not like moisture, and you want to help them as much as possible. Opening the oven door once or twice won't hurt your macarons. Make sure to bake the macarons for the time

specified in each recipe. There are very fine lines between underdone, perfect, and overdone macarons.

Coloring

If you want to add color to your macarons, the brand to use is ColorKitchen powdered dyes, which are great because they don't add moisture to the batter. I particularly like them because they are made with only natural ingredients and are derived from vegetables. If you're coloring the cookie part of your macaron, always add the dye to the dry ingredients, and sift it along with the almond flour and the powdered sugar. Do not add the color to the egg whites. If you want a really dark or bright macaron, and you add more than 1 teaspoon of dye to the recipe, be sure to reduce the powdered sugar by the same amount to maintain the proportions of dry to wet ingredients. For example, if you add 2 teaspoons blue dye, then reduce the powdered sugar by 2 teaspoons.

You can add color to the fillings very easily. Simply add the color to the mixture and combine it thoroughly. There is no need to remove any powdered sugar. Also, when adding color to the filling, a drop or two of water helps to bring out the colors, because ColorKitchen dyes are water-soluble. You can find all colors at colorkitchen foods.com.

Storing

In general, I think macarons should be made and eaten the same day. If you can't eat them all yourself, give them away to friends and family. Some people freeze macarons, but I don't recommend doing that. I think freezing and thawing them changes their texture. Macarons are special, and they should be treated that way.

This is the base recipe for a lot of the flavors in this chapter. You can turn these into sandwiches by filling them with Caramel Sauce (page 253), Butterscotch Sauce (page 249), Chocolate Ganache (page 257), or any other filling you can imagine. Top them with chopped peanuts, rainbow sprinkles, or finely shredded coconut. I hope you'll have fun finding new ways to fill and top these cookies.

Makes 60

3 large (102 grams) egg whites

1/4 cup plus 1 tablespoon (71 grams) cane sugar

1 teaspoon vanilla extract

1 1/4 cups plus 2 tablespoons (198 grams) powdered sugar

1 cup plus 2 tablespoons (113 grams) almond flour

>>> HIGH ALTITUDE—BAKE AT 350°F FOR 8 MINUTES.

Line 2 cookie sheets with parchment paper.

In the bowl of a stand mixer fitted with the whisk attachment, add the egg whites, cane sugar, and vanilla extract. Whisk, starting on low to avoid splattering, and slowly increasing the speed to high, until stiff peaks form.

Sift the powdered sugar and almond flour together into the bowl of meringue. Turn the mixer on low for 10 to 15 rotations until the dry ingredients start to blend into the meringue. Pulse the mixer on medium-high 4 to 5 times to incorporate the batter.

Remove the mixing bowl from the mixer, and gently stir the batter with a spatula just until there are no pockets of egg whites or dry bits of almond flour. Don't overstir. Transfer the batter to a piping bag fitted with Ateco tip #804.

Pipe the macaron batter onto the prepared cookie sheets (30 should fit on each cookie sheet). Holding a cookie sheet firmly in both hands, and making sure the parchment paper doesn't slide around, bang the cookie sheet on the counter a few times. Rotate the cookie sheet and bang it a few more times. Repeat with the other cookie sheet. This will smooth out the batter and will help form the macarons' famous "feet."

Let rest for 45 minutes, or until the rounds of batter have formed shells.

Preheat the oven to 350°F.

Bake for 10 minutes. Let cool completely on the cookie sheets.

Fill or serve immediately.

This is the second base recipe I use to create all the other varieties in this chapter. Just like the Vanilla Macarons, you can top or fill them with anything your heart desires. I like to fill them with Chocolate Fro-Yo (page 254) or mold a Caramel Candy (page 250) into a circle for the inside and sprinkle it with sea salt. I hope you have fun creating your own combinations.

Makes 60

3 large (102 grams) egg whites

1/4 cup plus 1 tablespoon (71 grams) cane sugar

1 teaspoon vanilla extract

1 1/4 cups (185 grams) powdered sugar

1 cup plus 2 tablespoons (113 grams) almond flour

3 tablespoons Dutch cocoa powder

>>> HIGH ALTITUDE—BAKE AT 350°F FOR 8 MINUTES.

Line 2 cookie sheets with parchment paper.

In the bowl of a stand mixer fitted with the whisk attachment, add the egg whites, cane sugar, and vanilla extract. Whisk, starting on low to avoid splattering, and slowly increasing the speed to high, until stiff peaks form.

Sift the powdered sugar, almond flour, and cocoa powder together into the bowl of meringue. Turn the mixer on low for 10 to 15 rotations until the dry ingredients start to blend into the meringue. Pulse the mixer on medium-high 4 to 5 times to incorporate the batter.

Remove the mixing bowl from the mixer, and gently stir the batter with a spatula just until there are no pockets of egg whites or dry bits of almond flour. Don't overstir. Transfer the batter to a piping bag fitted with Ateco tip #804.

Pipe the macaron batter onto the prepared cookie sheets (30 should fit on a cookie sheet). Holding a cookie sheet firmly in both hands, and making sure the parchment paper doesn't slide around, bang the cookie sheet on the counter a few times. Rotate the cookie sheet and bang it a few more times. Repeat with the other cookie sheet. This will smooth out the batter and will help form the macarons' famous "feet."

Let rest for 45 minutes, or until the rounds of batter have formed shells.

Preheat the oven to 350°F.

Bake for 10 minutes. Let cool completely on the cookie sheets.

Fill or serve immediately.

I love that I can make these macarons three different ways. If you prepare the recipe as written, with lemon flavor, they are sweet. If you substitute the juice of ½ a fresh lemon, they will be tarter. And if you use the juice of ½ a Meyer lemon, the taste is somewhere in between. For a person who loves lemons, this is the ultimate recipe.

Makes 30 sandwiches

BATTER

3 large (102 grams) egg whites

¼ cup plus 1 tablespoon (71 grams) cane sugar

1 teaspoon vanilla extract

1¼ cups plus 2 tablespoons (198 grams) powdered sugar

1 cup plus 2 tablespoons (113 grams) almond flour

FILLING

1 cup plus 3 tablespoons (170 grams) powdered sugar, sifted

6 tablespoons (85 grams) salted butter, softened

1 teaspoon lemon flavor

1 teaspoon water

¼ teaspoon ColorKitchen yellow dye (optional)

Line 2 cookie sheets with parchment paper.

To make the batter: In the bowl of a stand mixer fitted with the whisk attachment, add the egg whites, cane sugar, and vanilla extract. Whisk, starting on low to avoid splattering, and slowly increasing the speed to high, until stiff peaks form.

Sift the powdered sugar and almond flour together into the bowl of meringue. Turn the mixer on low for 10 to 15 rotations until the dry ingredients start to blend into the meringue. Pulse the mixer on medium-high 4 to 5 times to incorporate the batter.

Remove the mixing bowl from the mixer, and gently stir the batter with a spatula just until there are no pockets of egg whites or dry bits of almond flour. Don't overstir. Transfer the batter to a piping bag fitted with Ateco tip #804.

Pipe the macaron batter onto the prepared cookie sheets (30 should fit on each cookie sheet). Holding a cookie sheet firmly in both hands, and making sure the parchment paper doesn't slide around, bang the cookie sheet on the counter a few times. Rotate the cookie sheet and bang it a few more times. Repeat with the other cookie sheet. This will smooth out the batter and will help form the macarons' famous "feet."

Let rest for 45 minutes, or until the rounds of batter have formed shells.

Preheat the oven to 350°F.

Bake for 10 minutes. Let cool completely on the cookie sheets.

To make the filling: In the bowl of a stand mixer fitted

with the paddle attachment, add the powdered sugar, butter, lemon flavor, water, and yellow dye, if using. Mix on low until combined, increase the speed to high, and mix for 1 minute more, or until light and fluffy. Transfer to a piping bag with no tip.

Pair the macarons together by size, and turn over every other one. Pipe filling onto each turned-over macaron, and sandwich the pairs together.

Serve immediately.

>>> HIGH ALTITUDE—BAKE AT 350°F FOR 8 MINUTES.

Honey anything and I'm in! I love it so much that one year at the local pumpkin patch, a bee flew into the bag of cinnamon honey graham crackers that I was eating from, and I stuck my hand in the bag anyway because I just couldn't keep myself from eating more. It was the first and only time I've been stung by a bee—and it was worth it.

Makes 30 sandwiches

BATTER

3 large (102 grams) egg whites

1/4 cup plus 1 tablespoon (71 grams) cane sugar

1 teaspoon vanilla extract

1 1/4 cups plus 2 tablespoons (198 grams) powdered sugar

1 cup plus 2 tablespoons (113 grams) almond flour

1/2 teaspoon cinnamon

FILLING

1 cup plus 3 tablespoons (170 grams) powdered sugar, sifted

6 tablespoons (85 grams) salted butter, softened

1 tablespoon plus 1 teaspoon raw honey

1/2 teaspoon vanilla extract

Line 2 cookie sheets with parchment paper.

To make the batter: In the bowl of a stand mixer fitted with the whisk attachment, add the egg whites, cane sugar, and vanilla extract. Whisk, starting on low to avoid splattering, and slowly increasing the speed to high, until stiff peaks form.

Sift the powdered sugar, almond flour, and cinnamon together into the bowl of meringue. Turn the mixer on low for 10 to 15 rotations until the dry ingredients start to blend into the meringue. Pulse the mixer on medium-high 4 to 5 times to incorporate the batter.

Remove the mixing bowl from the mixer, and gently stir the batter with a spatula just until there are no pockets of egg whites or dry bits of almond flour. Don't overstir. Transfer the batter to a piping bag fitted with Ateco tip #804.

Pipe the macaron batter onto the prepared cookie sheets (30 should fit on each cookie sheet). Holding a cookie sheet firmly in both hands, and making sure the parchment paper doesn't slide around, bang the cookie sheet on the counter a few times. Rotate the cookie sheet and bang it a few more times. Repeat with the other cookie sheet. This will smooth out the batter and will help form the macarons' famous "feet."

Let rest for 45 minutes, or until the rounds of batter have formed shells.

Preheat the oven to 350°F.

Bake for 10 minutes. Let cool completely on the cookie sheets.

(continues)

To make the filling: In the bowl of a stand mixer fitted with the paddle attachment, add the powdered sugar, butter, honey, and vanilla extract. Mix on low until combined, increase the speed to high, and mix for 1 minute more, or until light and fluffy. Transfer to a piping bag with no tip.

Pair the macarons together by size, and turn over every other one. Pipe filling onto each turned-over macaron, and sandwich the pairs together.

Serve immediately.

>>> HIGH ALTITUDE—BAKE AT 350°F FOR 8 MINUTES.

You'd think that being a girl boss, working long hours, and getting up early, I would drink a lot of coffee, but I don't. Both my parents are big coffee drinkers—they drink multiple cups a day. But they always warned me away from following in their footsteps, so I never developed the coffee habit. Instead I enjoy my coffee flavor in my favorite desserts and cookies.

Makes 30 sandwiches

BATTER

3 large (102 grams) egg whites

$^1\!/_4$ cup plus 1 tablespoon (71 grams) cane sugar

1 teaspoon vanilla extract

$1^1\!/_4$ cups (185 grams) powdered sugar

1 cup plus 2 tablespoons (113 grams) almond flour

3 tablespoons Dutch cocoa powder

FILLING

1 cup plus 2 tablespoons (163 grams) powdered sugar, sifted

6 tablespoons (85 grams) salted butter, softened

1 tablespoon plus 1 teaspoon Dutch cocoa powder, sifted

2 teaspoons milk

1 teaspoon coffee flavor

Line 2 cookie sheets with parchment paper.

To make the batter: In the bowl of a stand mixer fitted with the whisk attachment, add the egg whites, cane sugar, and vanilla extract. Whisk, starting on low to avoid splattering, and slowly increasing the speed to high, until stiff peaks form.

Sift the powdered sugar, almond flour, and cocoa together into the bowl of meringue. Turn the mixer on low for 10 to 15 rotations until the dry ingredients start to blend into the meringue. Pulse the mixer on medium-high 4 to 5 times to incorporate the batter.

Remove the mixing bowl from the mixer, and gently stir the batter with a spatula just until there are no pockets of egg whites or dry bits of almond flour. Don't overstir. Transfer the batter to a piping bag fitted with Ateco tip #804.

Pipe the macaron batter onto the prepared cookie sheets (30 should fit on each cookie sheet). Holding a cookie sheet firmly in both hands, and making sure the parchment paper doesn't slide around, bang the cookie sheet on the counter a few times. Rotate the cookie sheet and bang it a few more times. Repeat with the other cookie sheet. This will smooth out the batter and will help form the macarons' famous "feet."

Let rest for 45 minutes, or until the rounds of batter have formed shells.

Preheat the oven to 350°F.

(continues)

Bake for 10 minutes. Let cool completely on the cookie sheets.

To make the filling: In the bowl of a stand mixer fitted with the paddle attachment, add the powdered sugar, butter, cocoa, milk, and coffee flavor. Mix on low until combined, increase the speed to high, and mix for 1 minute more, or until light and fluffy. Transfer to a piping bag with no tip.

Pair the macarons together by size, and turn over every other one. Pipe filling onto each turned-over macaron, and sandwich the pairs together.

Serve immediately.

>>> HIGH ALTITUDE—BAKE AT 350°F FOR 8 MINUTES.

Chocolate and peanut butter go together like cold milk and warm cookies.

Makes 30 sandwiches

BATTER

3 large (102 grams) egg whites

1/4 cup plus 1 tablespoon (71 grams) cane sugar

1 teaspoon vanilla extract

1 1/4 cups (185 grams) powdered sugar

1 cup plus 2 tablespoons (113 grams) almond flour

3 tablespoons Dutch cocoa powder

FILLING

1 cup plus 3 tablespoons (170 grams) powdered sugar, sifted

6 tablespoons (85 grams) salted butter, softened

Heaping 1 tablespoon peanut butter

2 teaspoons milk

1/2 teaspoon vanilla extract

Line 2 cookie sheets with parchment paper.

To make the batter: In the bowl of a stand mixer fitted with the whisk attachment, add the egg whites, cane sugar, and vanilla extract. Whisk, starting on low to avoid splattering, and slowly increasing the speed to high, until stiff peaks form.

Sift the powdered sugar, almond flour, and cocoa powder together into the bowl of meringue. Turn the mixer on low for 10 to 15 rotations until the dry ingredients start to blend into the meringue. Pulse the mixer on medium-high 4 to 5 times to incorporate the batter.

Remove the mixing bowl from the mixer, and gently stir the batter with a spatula just until there are no pockets of egg whites or dry bits of almond flour. Don't overstir. Transfer the batter to a piping bag fitted with Ateco tip #804.

Pipe the macaron batter onto the prepared cookie sheets (30 should fit on each cookie sheet). Holding a cookie sheet firmly in both hands, and making sure the parchment paper doesn't slide around, bang the cookie sheet on the counter a few times. Rotate the cookie sheet and bang it a few more times. Repeat with the other cookie sheet. This will smooth out the batter and will help form the macarons' famous "feet."

Let rest for 45 minutes, or until the rounds of batter have formed shells.

Preheat the oven to 350°F.

Bake for 10 minutes. Let cool completely on the cookie sheets.

To make the filling: In the bowl of a stand mixer fitted with the paddle attachment, add the powdered sugar, butter, peanut butter, milk, and vanilla extract. Mix on low until

(continues)

combined, increase the speed to high, and mix for 1 minute more, or until light and fluffy. Transfer to a piping bag with no tip.

Pair the macarons together by size, and turn over every other one. Pipe filling onto each turned-over macaron, and sandwich the pairs together.

Serve immediately.

>>> HIGH ALTITUDE—BAKE AT 350°F FOR 8 MINUTES.

As a child deprived of sweets, you know I loved pistachios so much that I would choose them over gummy worms at the bulk candy store. These Pistachio French Macarons will always be one of my favorites, and you can be happy I didn't love gummy worms more or this recipe would be very, very different.

Makes 30 sandwiches

BATTER

3 large (102 grams) egg whites

$\frac{1}{4}$ cup plus 1 tablespoon (71 grams) cane sugar

1 teaspoon vanilla extract

$1\frac{1}{4}$ cups plus 2 tablespoons (198 grams) powdered sugar

1 cup plus 2 tablespoons (113 grams) almond flour

$\frac{1}{4}$ cup (35 grams) roasted, salted, shelled pistachios, finely chopped

FILLING

1 cup plus 3 tablespoons (170 grams) powdered sugar, sifted

6 tablespoons (85 grams) salted butter, softened

1 teaspoon water

$\frac{1}{2}$ teaspoon pistachio extract

$\frac{1}{8}$ teaspoon ColorKitchen yellow dye (optional)

$\frac{1}{8}$ teaspoon ColorKitchen blue dye (optional)

Line 2 cookie sheets with parchment paper.

To make the batter: In the bowl of a stand mixer fitted with the whisk attachment, add the egg whites, cane sugar, and vanilla extract. Whisk, starting on low to avoid splattering, and slowly increasing the speed to high, until stiff peaks form.

Sift the powdered sugar and almond flour together into the bowl of meringue. Turn the mixer on low for 10 to 15 rotations until the dry ingredients start to blend into the meringue. Pulse the mixer on medium-high 4 to 5 times to incorporate the batter.

Remove the mixing bowl from the mixer, and gently stir the batter with a spatula just until there are no pockets of egg whites or dry bits of almond flour. Don't overstir. Transfer the batter to a piping bag fitted with Ateco tip #804.

Pipe the macaron batter onto the prepared cookie sheets (30 should fit on a cookie sheet). Holding a cookie sheet firmly in both hands, and making sure the parchment paper doesn't slide around, bang the cookie sheet on the counter a few times. Rotate the cookie sheet and bang it a few more times. Repeat with the other cookie sheet. This will smooth out the batter and will help form the macarons' famous "feet." Sprinkle pistachios on top of each macaron.

Let rest for 45 minutes, or until the rounds of batter have formed shells.

Preheat the oven to 350°F.

Bake for 10 minutes. Let cool completely on the cookie sheets.

(continues)

To make the filling: In the bowl of a stand mixer fitted with the paddle attachment, add the powdered sugar, butter, water, pistachio extract, and the yellow and blue dye, if using. Mix on low until combined, increase the speed to high, and mix for 1 minute more, or until light and fluffy. Transfer to a piping bag with no tip.

Pair the macarons together by size, and turn over every other one. Pipe filling onto each turned-over macaron, and sandwich the pairs together.

Serve immediately.

>>> HIGH ALTITUDE—BAKE AT 350°F FOR 8 MINUTES.

As you've probably figured out by now, coconut will always be one of my favorite flavors. It's so light, perfectly sweet, and delicious. When new employees tell me they don't like coconut, I have them try one of our coconut desserts, and they change their minds every time, because we use unsweetened coconut. Coconut French Macarons are the best coconut dessert I've ever made, period.

Makes 30 sandwiches

BATTER

3 large (102 grams) egg whites

1/4 cup plus 1 tablespoon (71 grams) cane sugar

1 teaspoon vanilla extract

1 1/4 cups plus 2 tablespoons (198 grams) powdered sugar

1 cup plus 2 tablespoons (113 grams) almond flour

1/3 cup (30 grams) unsweetened finely shredded coconut

FILLING

1 cup plus 3 tablespoons (170 grams) powdered sugar, sifted

6 tablespoons (85 grams) salted butter, softened

1 to 2 teaspoons milk

1/2 teaspoon coconut extract

Line 2 cookie sheets with parchment paper.

To make the batter: In the bowl of a stand mixer fitted with the whisk attachment, add the egg whites, cane sugar, and vanilla extract. Whisk, starting on low to avoid splattering, and slowly increasing the speed to high, until stiff peaks form.

Sift the powdered sugar and almond flour together into the bowl of meringue. Turn the mixer on low for 10 to 15 rotations until the dry ingredients start to blend into the meringue. Pulse the mixer on medium-high 4 to 5 times to incorporate the batter.

Remove the mixing bowl from the mixer, and gently stir the batter with a spatula just until there are no pockets of egg whites or dry bits of almond flour. Don't overstir. Transfer the batter to a piping bag fitted with Ateco tip #804.

Pipe the macaron batter onto the prepared cookie sheets (30 should fit on each cookie sheet). Holding a cookie sheet firmly in both hands, and making sure the parchment paper doesn't slide around, bang the cookie sheet on the counter a few times. Rotate the cookie sheet and bang it a few more times. Repeat with the other cookie sheet. This will smooth out the batter and will help form the macarons' famous "feet." Sprinkle coconut on top of each macaron.

Let rest for 45 minutes, or until the rounds of batter have formed a shell.

Preheat the oven to 350°F.

Bake for 10 minutes. Let cool completely on the cookie sheets.

(continues)

To make the filling: In the bowl of a stand mixer fitted with the paddle attachment, add the powdered sugar, butter, milk, and coconut extract. Mix on low until combined, increase the speed to high, and mix for 1 minute more, or until light and fluffy. Transfer to a piping bag with no tip.

Pair the macarons together by size, and turn over every other one. Pipe filling onto each turned-over macaron, and sandwich the pairs together.

Serve immediately.

>>> HIGH ALTITUDE—BAKE AT 350°F FOR 8 MINUTES.

Chocolate chip cookies are the most beloved cookie there is, but I'll bet you've never seen a chocolate chip macaron—until now. You're welcome.

Makes 30 sandwiches

BATTER

3 large (102 grams) egg whites

$1/4$ cup plus 1 tablespoon (71 grams) cane sugar

1 teaspoon vanilla extract

$1^1/4$ cups plus 2 tablespoons (198 grams) powdered sugar

1 cup plus 2 tablespoons (113 grams) almond flour

3 tablespoons finely chopped milk chocolate

FILLING

1 cup plus 1 tablespoon (155 grams) powdered sugar, sifted

6 tablespoons (85 grams) salted butter, softened

3 tablespoons Dutch cocoa powder, sifted

2 teaspoons milk

Line 2 cookie sheets with parchment paper.

To make the batter: In the bowl of a stand mixer fitted with the whisk attachment, add the egg whites, cane sugar, and vanilla extract. Whisk, starting on low to avoid splattering, and slowly increasing the speed to high, until stiff peaks form.

Sift the powdered sugar and almond flour together into the bowl of meringue. Turn the mixer on low for 10 to 15 rotations until the dry ingredients start to blend into the meringue. Pulse the mixer on medium-high 4 to 5 times to incorporate the batter.

Remove the mixing bowl from the mixer, and gently stir the batter with a spatula just until there are no pockets of egg whites or dry bits of almond flour. Don't overstir. Transfer the batter to a piping bag fitted with Ateco tip #804.

Pipe the macaron batter onto the prepared cookie sheets (30 should fit on each cookie sheet). Holding a cookie sheet firmly in both hands, and making sure the parchment paper doesn't slide around, bang the cookie sheet on the counter a few times. Rotate the cookie sheet and bang it a few more times. Repeat with the other cookie sheet. This will smooth out the batter and will help form the macarons' famous "feet." Sprinkle the chopped chocolate on top of each macaron.

Let rest for 45 minutes, or until the rounds of batter have formed shells.

Preheat the oven to 350°F.

(continues)

Bake for 10 minutes. Let cool completely on the cookie sheets.

To make the filling: In the bowl of a stand mixer fitted with the paddle attachment, add the powdered sugar, butter, cocoa powder, and milk. Mix on low until combined, increase the speed to high, and mix for 1 minute more, or until light and fluffy. Transfer to a piping bag with no tip.

Pair the macarons together by size, and turn over every other one. Pipe filling onto each turned-over macaron, and sandwich the pairs together.

Serve immediately.

>>> HIGH ALTITUDE—BAKE AT 350°F FOR 8 MINUTES.

TRIPLE CHOCOLATE FRENCH MACARONS

There's nothing better than chocolate…unless you add more chocolate. That's just my opinion. Chocolate macaron, chocolate ganache, and chocolate buttercream combine to elevate this recipe to cookie nirvana.

Makes 30 sandwiches

BATTER

3 large (102 grams) egg whites

1/4 cup plus 1 tablespoon (71 grams) cane sugar

1 teaspoon vanilla extract

1 1/4 cups (185 grams) powdered sugar

1 cup plus 2 tablespoons (113 grams) almond flour

3 tablespoons Dutch cocoa powder

FILLING

1 cup plus 1 tablespoon (155 grams) powdered sugar, sifted

6 tablespoons (85 grams) salted butter, softened

3 tablespoons Dutch cocoa powder, sifted

2 teaspoons milk

1/3 cup Chocolate Ganache (page 257)

Line 2 cookie sheets with parchment paper.

To make the batter: In the bowl of a stand mixer fitted with the whisk attachment, add the egg whites, cane sugar, and vanilla extract. Whisk, starting on low to avoid splattering, and slowly increasing the speed to high, until stiff peaks form.

Sift the powdered sugar, almond flour, and cocoa together into the bowl of meringue. Turn the mixer on low for 10 to 15 rotations until the dry ingredients start to blend into the meringue. Pulse the mixer on medium-high 4 to 5 times to incorporate the batter.

Remove the mixing bowl from the mixer, and gently stir the batter with a spatula just until there are no pockets of egg whites or dry bits of almond flour. Don't overstir. Transfer the batter to a piping bag fitted with Ateco tip #804.

Pipe the macaron batter onto the prepared cookie sheets (30 should fit on each cookie sheet). Holding a cookie sheet firmly in both hands, and making sure the parchment paper doesn't slide around, bang the cookie sheet on the counter a few times. Rotate the cookie sheet and bang it a few more times. Repeat with the other cookie sheet. This will smooth out the batter and will help form the macarons' famous "feet."

Let rest for 45 minutes, or until the rounds of batter have formed shells.

Preheat the oven to 350°F.

Bake for 10 minutes. Let cool completely on the cookie sheets.

To make the filling: In the bowl of a stand mixer fitted

with the paddle attachment, add the powdered sugar, butter, cocoa, and milk. Mix on low until combined, increase the speed to high, and mix for 1 minute more, or until light and fluffy. Transfer the filling to a piping bag with no tip.

Load the chocolate ganache into another piping bag fitted with Ateco tip #56.

Pair the macarons together by size, and turn over every other one. Pipe a circle of ganache around the edge of each turned-over macaron. Pipe a dollop of filling into the center of each turned-over macaron. Sandwich the pairs together.

Serve immediately.

>>> HIGH ALTITUDE—BAKE AT 350°F FOR 8 MINUTES.

Mint is refreshing, and I feel happy when I eat it. I even painted the walls of Dessert'D mint colored so I could be surrounded by it every single day. Mixing mint with chocolate only makes it better.

Makes 30 sandwiches

BATTER

3 large (102 grams) egg whites

1/4 cup plus 1 tablespoon (71 grams) cane sugar

1 teaspoon vanilla extract

1 1/4 cups (185 grams) powdered sugar

1 cup plus 2 tablespoons (113 grams) almond flour

3 tablespoons Dutch cocoa powder

FILLING

1 cup plus 3 tablespoons (170 grams) powdered sugar, sifted

6 tablespoons (85 grams) salted butter, softened

1 teaspoon water

1/2 teaspoon peppermint flavor

1/8 teaspoon ColorKitchen blue dye (optional)

1/8 teaspoon ColorKitchen yellow dye (optional)

1/3 cup Chocolate Ganache (page 257)

Line 2 cookie sheets with parchment paper.

To make the batter: In the bowl of a stand mixer fitted with the whisk attachment, add the egg whites, cane sugar, and vanilla extract. Whisk, starting on low to avoid splattering, and slowly increasing the speed to high, until stiff peaks form.

Sift the powdered sugar, almond flour, and cocoa together into the bowl of meringue. Turn the mixer on low for 10 to 15 rotations until the dry ingredients start to blend into the meringue. Pulse the mixer on medium-high 4 to 5 times to incorporate the batter.

Remove the mixing bowl from the mixer, and gently stir the batter with a spatula just until there are no pockets of egg whites or dry bits of almond flour. Don't overstir. Transfer the batter to a piping bag fitted with Ateco tip #804.

Pipe the macaron batter onto the prepared cookie sheets (30 should fit on each cookie sheet). Holding a cookie sheet firmly in both hands, and making sure the parchment paper doesn't slide around, bang the cookie sheet on the counter a few times. Rotate the cookie sheet and bang it a few more times. Repeat with the other cookie sheet. This will smooth out the batter and will help form the macarons' famous "feet."

Let rest for 45 minutes, or until the rounds of batter have formed shells.

Preheat the oven to 350°F.

Bake for 10 minutes. Let cool completely on the cookie sheets.

To make the filling: In the bowl of a stand mixer fitted

(continues)

with the paddle attachment, add the powdered sugar, butter, water, peppermint flavor, and blue and yellow dyes, if using. Mix on low until combined, increase the speed to high, and mix for 1 minute more, or until light and fluffy. Transfer the filling to a piping bag with no tip.

Load the chocolate ganache into another piping bag fitted with Ateco tip #56.

Pair the macarons together by size, and turn over every other one. Pipe a circle of ganache around the edge of each turned-over macaron. Pipe a dollop of filling into the center of each turned-over macaron. Sandwich the pairs together.

Serve immediately.

>>> HIGH ALTITUDE—BAKE AT 350°F FOR 8 MINUTES.

This is one of the biggest sellers at the bakery, and it's obvious why. There are few things as delicious as salted caramel. Add it to France's finest cookie, and the result will inevitably be popular. This sweet and salty combo never gets old.

Makes 30 sandwiches

BATTER

3 large (102 grams) egg whites

$\frac{1}{4}$ cup plus 1 tablespoon (71 grams) cane sugar

1 teaspoon vanilla extract

$1\frac{1}{4}$ cups plus 2 tablespoons (198 grams) powdered sugar

1 cup plus 2 tablespoons (113 grams) almond flour

TOPPING

1 teaspoon fine sea salt

1 teaspoon cane sugar

FILLING

1 cup plus 3 tablespoons (170 grams) powdered sugar, sifted

6 tablespoons (85 grams) salted butter, softened

1 tablespoon plus $\frac{1}{3}$ cup Caramel Sauce (page 253), divided

Line 2 cookie sheets with parchment paper.

To make the batter: In the bowl of a stand mixer fitted with the whisk attachment, add the egg whites, cane sugar, and vanilla extract. Whisk, starting on low to avoid splattering, and slowly increasing to high, until stiff peaks form.

Sift the powdered sugar and almond flour together into the bowl of meringue. Turn the mixer on low for 10 to 15 rotations until the dry ingredients start to blend into the meringue. Pulse the mixer on medium-high 4 to 5 times to incorporate the batter.

Remove the mixing bowl from the mixer, and gently stir the batter with a spatula just until there are no pockets of egg whites or dry bits of almond flour. Don't overstir. Transfer the batter to a piping bag fitted with Ateco tip #804.

Pipe the macaron batter onto the prepared cookie sheets (30 should fit on each cookie sheet). Holding a cookie sheet firmly in both hands, and making sure the parchment paper doesn't slide around, bang the cookie sheet on the counter a few times. Rotate the cookie sheet and bang it a few more times. Repeat with the other cookie sheet. This will smooth out the batter and will help form the macarons' famous "feet."

Let rest for 45 minutes, or until the rounds of batter have formed shells.

Preheat the oven to 350°F.

Bake for 10 minutes. Let cool completely on the cookie sheets.

To make the topping: Mix the sea salt and cane sugar together in a small dish. Set aside.

To make the filling: In the bowl of a stand mixer fitted with the paddle attachment, add the powdered sugar, butter, and 1 tablespoon caramel sauce. Mix on low until combined, increase the speed to high, and mix for 1 minute more, or until light and fluffy. Transfer to a piping bag with no tip.

Load the remaining ⅓ cup caramel sauce into another piping bag fitted with Ateco tip #56.

Pair the macarons together by size and turn over every other one. Pipe a circle of caramel sauce around the edge of each turned-over macaron. Sprinkle the sea salt mixture over the circles of caramel sauce.

Pipe a dollop of filling into the center of each turned-over macaron, and sandwich the pairs together.

Serve immediately.

>>> HIGH ALTITUDE—BAKE AT 350°F FOR 8 MINUTES.

Blueberries have always been my favorite fruit. Something about their sweet flavor makes them taste more like candy than fruit to me. Though I like to use fresh berries when I can, this recipe works just as well with frozen, which make these macarons accessible all year long.

Makes 30 sandwiches

BATTER

3 large (102 grams) egg whites

1/4 cup plus 1 tablespoon (71 grams) cane sugar

1 teaspoon vanilla extract

1 1/4 cups plus 2 tablespoons (198 grams) powdered sugar

1 cup plus 2 tablespoons (113 grams) almond flour

1 teaspoon ColorKitchen blue dye (optional)

SYRUP AND COMPOTE

Heaping 3/4 cup (142 grams) blueberries, fresh or frozen

1/4 cup (57 grams) cane sugar

1/4 cup water

FILLING

3/4 cup plus 1 tablespoon (113 grams) powdered sugar, sifted

4 tablespoons (57 grams) salted butter, softened

1 tablespoon blueberry syrup (see above)

Line 2 cookie sheets with parchment paper.

To make the batter: In the bowl of a stand mixer fitted with the whisk attachment, add the egg whites, cane sugar, and vanilla extract. Whisk, starting on low to avoid splattering, and slowly increasing the speed to high, until stiff peaks form.

Sift the powdered sugar, almond flour, and blue dye, if using, together into the bowl of meringue. Turn the mixer on low for 10 to 15 rotations until the dry ingredients start to blend into the meringue. Pulse the mixer on medium-high 4 to 5 times to incorporate the batter.

Remove the mixing bowl from the mixer, and gently stir the batter with a spatula just until there are no pockets of egg whites or dry bits of almond flour. Don't overstir. Transfer the batter to a piping bag fitted with Ateco tip #804.

Pipe the macaron batter onto the prepared cookie sheets (30 should fit on each cookie sheet). Holding a cookie sheet firmly in both hands, and making sure the parchment paper doesn't slide around, bang the cookie sheet on the counter a few times. Rotate the cookie sheet and bang it a few more times. Repeat with the other cookie sheet. This will smooth out the batter and will help form the macarons' famous "feet."

Let rest for 45 minutes, or until the rounds of batter have formed shells.

To make the blueberry syrup and compote: In a medium pot, combine the blueberries, cane sugar, and water. Cook over medium heat until the blueberries start to burst and the mixture has reduced by half. Remove from the heat.

(continues)

Transfer 1 tablespoon of the blueberry syrup to a mixing bowl, and set aside for use in the filling. Refrigerate the compote for at least 15 minutes, until cold throughout.

Preheat the oven to 350°F.

Bake the macarons for 10 minutes. Let cool completely on the cookie sheets.

To make the filling: In the bowl of a stand mixer fitted with the paddle attachment, add the powdered sugar, butter, and blueberry syrup. Mix on low until combined, increase the speed to high, and mix for 1 minute more, or until light and fluffy. Transfer to a piping bag fitted with Ateco tip #10.

Pair the macarons together by size, and turn over every other one. Pipe a circle of filling around the border of each turned-over macaron. Fill the inside of the circle with a dollop of blueberry compote (about ½ teaspoon). Sandwich the pairs together.

Serve immediately.

>>> HIGH ALTITUDE—BAKE AT 350°F FOR 8 MINUTES.

On special summer days my parents took us to the iconic Rainbow Cone, in my hometown of Chicago, where sometimes I would order a banana split. I've never found another banana split to compete with the one from Rainbow Cone, so when my craving hits I bake these macarons instead.

Makes 30 sandwiches

VANILLA BATTER

1$^1/_2$ large (51 grams) egg whites

2$^1/_2$ tablespoons cane sugar

$^1/_2$ teaspoon vanilla extract

$^1/_2$ cup plus 3 tablespoons (99 grams) powdered sugar

$^1/_2$ cup plus 1 tablespoon (57 grams) almond flour

Rainbow sprinkles

CHOCOLATE BATTER

1$^1/_2$ large (51 grams) egg whites

2$^1/_2$ tablespoons cane sugar

$^1/_2$ teaspoon vanilla extract

$^1/_2$ cup plus 2 tablespoons (92 grams) powdered sugar

$^1/_2$ cup plus 1 tablespoon (57 grams) almond flour

1$^1/_2$ tablespoons Dutch cocoa powder

FILLING

$^3/_4$ cup plus 1 tablespoon (113 grams) powdered sugar, sifted

4 tablespoons (57 grams) salted butter, softened

$^1/_2$ teaspoon banana flavor

$^1/_2$ teaspoon ColorKitchen yellow dye (optional)

$^1/_2$ teaspoon water

$^1/_3$ cup Strawberry Preserves (page 266)

$^1/_3$ cup Chocolate Ganache (page 257)

Line 2 cookie sheets with parchment paper.

To make the vanilla batter: In the bowl of a stand mixer fitted with the whisk attachment, add the egg whites, cane sugar, and vanilla extract. Whisk, starting on low to avoid splattering, and slowly increasing the speed to high, until stiff peaks form.

Sift the powdered sugar and almond flour together into the bowl of meringue. Turn the mixer on low for 10 to 15 rotations until the dry ingredients start to blend into the meringue. Pulse the mixer on medium-high 4 to 5 times to incorporate the batter.

Remove the mixing bowl from the mixer, and gently stir the batter with a spatula just until there are no pockets of egg whites or dry bits of almond flour. Don't overstir. Transfer the batter to a piping bag fitted with Ateco tip #804.

Pipe the macaron batter onto one of the prepared cookie sheets (30 should fit on each cookie sheet). Holding the cookie sheet firmly in both hands, and making sure the

(continues)

parchment paper doesn't slide around, bang the cookie sheet on the counter a few times. Rotate the cookie sheet and bang it a few more times. This will smooth out the batter and will help form the macarons' famous "feet." Sprinkle the tops with rainbow sprinkles.

Let rest for 45 minutes, or until the rounds of batter have formed shells.

To make the chocolate batter: Follow the same instructions as for the vanilla batter, sifting the cocoa into the meringue with the powdered sugar and almond flour. Pipe rounds of batter onto the second cookie sheet, bang it on the counter a few times, and let rest for 45 minutes, or until the rounds of batter have formed shells.

Preheat the oven to 350°F.

Bake for 10 minutes. Let cool completely on the cookie sheets.

To make the filling: In the bowl of a stand mixer fitted with the paddle attachment, add the powdered sugar, butter, banana flavor, yellow dye (if using), and water. Mix on low until combined, increase the speed to high, and mix for 1 minute more, or until light and fluffy. Transfer to a piping bag fitted with Ateco tip #10.

Turn over the chocolate macarons, and pair each one with a vanilla macaron. Pipe a circle of filling around the border of each chocolate macaron. Fill the inside of the circle with strawberry preserves (about ½ teaspoon). Drizzle chocolate ganache on top, and sandwich with the vanilla macarons.

Serve immediately.

>>> HIGH ALTITUDE—BAKE AT 350°F FOR 8 MINUTES.

COOKIE NECESSITIES

IN THIS CHAPTER YOU WILL FIND all the things you need to elevate your cookies: recipes for Caramel Sauce (page 253) and Cookie Glaze (page 262), instructions for tempering chocolate, and much more. I've included a few extra recipes for sweets that go really well with cookies, like Chocolate Fro-Yo (page 254) and Strawberry Milk (page 265).

At Dessert'D we keep most of these items on hand all the time. Make a few of them ahead, and they will always be waiting in the pantry or the refrigerator. Then you'll be ready to create your own combinations—like adding Butterscotch Sauce (page 249) to Coconut French Macarons (page 223). Next time you are planning a party, set up a cookie bar. Put out a selection of sauces and ice creams from this chapter along with a variety of cookies, and let everyone create their own pairings. Go wild!

Brown butter can take your recipe from good to simply amazing. People will try to figure out what "that flavor" is or why "it just tastes so good." That is the allure of brown butter. The flavor may be hard to describe, but I like to say it's somewhere between sweet, caramel, maple, and nutty—all in one bite.

Makes a little over ⅓ cup (85 grams)

½ cup (113 grams) salted butter

In a medium pot over medium heat, cook the butter, stirring occasionally with a heatproof spatula, until it starts to bubble. If it becomes so bubbly that it turns white, making it hard to see the color of the butter, remove it from the heat and stir until the bubbles calm down. Return it to the heat, and keep cooking until the butter turns the color of maple syrup and smells nutty and sweet. The milk solids will sink, which is another indication of doneness. The entire process can take as long as 5 to 10 minutes. Be patient, but watch carefully, because it can burn quickly.

Remove the pot from the heat, and immediately scrape the butter into a mixing bowl, making sure to get every last delicious bit.

Let cool to room temperature before using in recipes.

>>> HIGH ALTITUDE—FOLLOW THE RECIPE AS NOTED.

BROWN SUGAR

Once I learned how easy it is to make brown sugar, I never bought it again. Who knew that mixing cane sugar with a little molasses was all it takes? When you prepare it yourself you get to control the level of darkness—and the darker it is, the more flavor it has. You can make as little or as much as you want. Feel free to cut this recipe in half if you don't think you'll go through it fast enough, but it will last way longer than any brown sugar you'll buy—and it tastes better, too!

Makes 1 pound (454 grams)

2 cups (454 grams) cane sugar

¼ cup (79 grams) Wholesome Molasses

In the bowl of a stand mixer fitted with the paddle attachment, mix the sugar and molasses on low until combined into a dark brown sugar. Scrape down the sides of the bowl, and mix again to be sure the molasses and sugar are completely combined.

Store in an airtight container for up to 6 months.

>>> HIGH ALTITUDE—FOLLOW THE RECIPE AS NOTED.

BUTTERSCOTCH SAUCE

I absolutely love anything butterscotch. This sweet and salty sauce is perfect for adding to frostings, dipping cookies or biscotti, or just eating with a spoon!

Makes 18 ounces (510 grams)

1 cup (226 grams) cane sugar

1/4 cup (57 grams) salted butter, softened

2 teaspoons Wholesome Molasses

1 cup (237 milliliters) heavy whipping cream

1/2 teaspoon vanilla extract

1/2 teaspoon fine sea salt

In a medium pot, combine the sugar, butter, and molasses, and cook over medium heat, stirring frequently with a high-heat spatula, until completely combined and smooth.

Add the cream slowly, stirring constantly.

Simmer for 4 to 5 minutes, until the mixture starts to bubble up and rise a little. Remove from the heat.

Add the vanilla extract and the sea salt, and stir to combine completely.

Store in a glass jar or squeeze bottle in the refrigerator for up to 2 weeks. Let warm to room temperature before using.

>>> HIGH ALTITUDE—FOLLOW THE RECIPE AS NOTED.

This recipe makes the chewy caramels that are used in recipes such as Apple Pie Cookies (page 41) and Salted Caramel Chocolate Chip Cookies (page 38). Make them ahead so they are ready to add to the recipes, or just grab a few and eat them by themselves. If making to eat on their own, sprinkle sea salt on top or add nuts for different variations. With only three ingredients, they are pretty simple.

Makes about 30

1¹/₂ cups (340 grams) cane sugar

¹/₂ cup (113 grams) salted butter, softened

¹/₂ cup (118 milliliters) heavy whipping cream

In a medium pot over medium heat, cook the sugar, stirring with a high-heat spatula to keep it from burning. The sugar on the bottom will melt and turn golden-brown; stir to bring it to the top and allow the remaining sugar to sink. Clumps will form before the sugar turns into a liquid. As the sugar liquefies, stir it frequently to prevent burning.

When the sugar has completely melted and there are no remaining chunks, add the butter. Be careful—steam will rise up quickly. Continue to cook, stirring constantly, until the butter has completely melted.

Add the cream a little at a time. Be careful, because the cream is colder than the sugar mixture, so more steam will rise up quickly. Stir constantly after each addition until completely combined. After about half the cream is added, you can add it more quickly.

Remove the caramel from the heat. Pour through a strainer into a bowl to remove any clumps.

Pour the caramel into ¹/₂-ounce candy molds, and let set at room temperature overnight.

Remove the candies from the molds and use immediately, or wrap in waxed paper and store at room temperature or in the refrigerator for up to 2 weeks.

>>> HIGH ALTITUDE—FOLLOW THE RECIPE AS NOTED.

I never liked caramel. That is, until I started making my own. That's when I realized that most caramel isn't true caramel. It often contains unnecessary ingredients like water and corn syrup, or it may include "caramel flavoring," which I definitely don't like. This sauce gets its flavor from actually caramelizing the sugar. It's so good and so easy to make, you'll wonder why you ever bought a caramel sauce.

Makes 30 ounces (850 grams)

2 cups (454 grams) cane sugar

1/2 cup (113 grams) salted butter

2 cups (473 milliliters) heavy whipping cream

In a medium pot over medium heat, cook the sugar, stirring with a high-heat spatula to keep it from burning. The sugar on the bottom will melt and turn golden-brown; stir to bring it to the top and allow the remaining sugar to sink. Clumps will form before the sugar turns into a liquid. As the sugar liquefies, stir it frequently to prevent burning.

When the sugar has completely melted and there are no remaining chunks, add the butter. Be careful—steam will rise up quickly. Continue to cook, stirring constantly, until the butter has completely melted.

Add the cream a little at a time. Be careful, because the cream is colder than the sugar mixture, so more steam will rise up quickly. Stir constantly after each addition until completely combined. After about half the cream is added, you can add it more quickly.

Remove the caramel from the heat. Pour through a strainer into a bowl to remove any clumps. Let cool completely before using.

Store in a glass jar or squeeze bottle in the refrigerator for up to 2 weeks. Let warm to room temperature before using.

>>> HIGH ALTITUDE—FOLLOW THE RECIPE AS NOTED.

Frozen yogurt will forever and always be my favorite frozen dessert, and chocolate is the best flavor. In my mind it doesn't get any better than this—unless you add a cookie on top.

Makes 1¼ quarts

2 cups (473 milliliters) milk

¾ cup (170 grams) cane sugar

⅓ cup (30 grams) Dutch cocoa powder

16 ounces (454 grams) plain yogurt

1 teaspoon vanilla extract

In a medium pot, combine the milk, sugar, and cocoa, and cook over high heat until the sugar has dissolved and the temperature has reached 140°F. Remove from the heat.

Place the pot in the refrigerator, and let the mixture chill overnight. Place the bowl of an ice cream maker and a 9 x 5-inch loaf pan in the freezer overnight.

The next day, remove the milk mixture from the refrigerator, add the yogurt and vanilla extract, and whisk to combine completely.

Place the bowl of the ice cream maker on the machine, and turn it on low (with nothing in it yet). Slowly pour the mixture into the bowl, and churn for 25 to 30 minutes (or follow the instructions for your ice cream maker). Transfer the frozen yogurt to the loaf pan, and spread evenly. Freeze overnight before serving.

>>> HIGH ALTITUDE—FOLLOW THE RECIPE AS NOTED.

CHOCOLATE GANACHE

Ganache is a thick chocolate sauce made from melted chocolate and cream. Use it as a sauce or for dipping biscotti or drizzling over cookies.

Makes 14 ounces (397 grams)

½ cup plus 2 tablespoons (85 grams) chopped dark chocolate

½ cup plus 2 tablespoons (85 grams) chopped milk chocolate

1 cup (236 milliliters) heavy whipping cream

Place both chocolates in a heatproof bowl. Place the bowl over a medium pot half filled with simmering water, making sure the bowl does not touch the water.

When the chocolate is melted, slowly add the cream, stirring constantly, until completely combined with the chocolate. Let cool to room temperature before using.

Store in a glass jar or squeeze bottle in the refrigerator for up to 1 week. Let warm to room temperature before using.

>>> HIGH ALTITUDE—FOLLOW THE RECIPE AS NOTED.

CHOLATE MILK

There's nothing better than milk and cookies...unless it's chocolate milk and cookies!

Makes 16 fluid ounces (473 milliliters)

2 cups (473 milliliters) milk

1/4 cup (57 grams) cane sugar

6 tablespoons (52 grams)
chopped milk chocolate

2 tablespoons Dutch cocoa
powder

In a medium pot, combine all the ingredients, and cook over high heat, whisking constantly, until the ingredients have melted, the mixture is smooth, and the temperature has reached 140°F.

Transfer to a glass bottle with a lid (so you can shake it later, because the chocolate will separate). Place in the refrigerator until cold, at least 6 hours or overnight.

To serve, shake vigorously, and pour into glasses.

Store in the refrigerator for up to 7 days.

>>> HIGH ALTITUDE—FOLLOW THE RECIPE AS NOTED.

When I first opened Dessert'D, I made frozen yogurt and vegan ice cream from scratch daily. Making ice cream and fro-yo on a large scale is a lot of work. But making small batches at home is the most fun I've ever had. And if I'm not making Chocolate Fro-Yo (page 254), I'm making this recipe, my next favorite. Especially if I happen to have Sea Salt Dark Chocolate Chunk Cookies (page 50) lying around…yep, I make ice cream sandwiches.

Makes 1 quart

2 cups (473 milliliters) unsweetened vanilla coconut milk

1/2 cup (113 grams) cane sugar

1 13.5-ounce can heavy coconut cream

1/2 teaspoon coconut extract

In a medium pot, combine the coconut milk and sugar, and cook over high heat until the sugar has dissolved and the temperature has reached 140°F. Remove from the heat.

Place the pot in the refrigerator, and let the mixture chill overnight. Place the bowl of an ice cream maker and a 9 x 5-inch loaf pan in the freezer overnight.

The next day, remove the coconut milk mixture from the fridge, and whisk in the coconut cream and the coconut extract until completely combined.

Place the bowl of the ice cream maker on the machine, and turn it on low (with nothing in it yet). Slowly pour in the mixture, and churn for 25 to 30 minutes (or follow the instructions for your ice cream maker). Transfer the ice cream to the loaf pan and spread evenly. Freeze overnight before serving.

>>> HIGH ALTITUDE—FOLLOW THE RECIPE AS NOTED.

COOKIE GLAZE

My mom taught me this recipe, which she called "frosting," when I was thirteen. I have renamed it now that I know a thing or two about baking. I've perfected it over time, but I didn't need to change it very much.

Makes about 14 ounces (397 grams)

Heaping 2¹/₃ cups (340 grams) powdered sugar, sifted

¹/₄ cup (59 milliliters) milk

VARIATIONS

Banana—add 1 teaspoon banana flavor

Coconut—add ¹/₂ teaspoon coconut extract

Lemon—add 1 teaspoon lemon flavor

Orange—add ¹/₂ teaspoon orange flavor

Cherry—add 1 teaspoon cherry flavor

Almond—add 1 teaspoon almond flavor

Peppermint—add ¹/₂ teaspoon peppermint flavor

Butterscotch—add 2 tablespoons Butterscotch Sauce (page 249)

Caramel—add 2 tablespoons Caramel Sauce (page 253)

In a medium mixing bowl, whisk together the powdered sugar and milk (and the flavor or extract, if using) until smooth. Use immediately.

>>> VEGAN—REPLACE THE MILK WITH UNSWEETENED VANILLA COCONUT MILK OR WATER.

I didn't know that strawberry milk existed until I was an adult. I grew up with plain milk or chocolate milk, and I had no idea that I could have been drinking a sweet pastel-pink milk for so many years. I'm making up for it now.

Makes 16 fluid ounces (473 milliliters)

2 cups (473 milliliters) milk

1/4 cup plus 2 tablespoons Strawberry Preserves (page 266)

Combine the milk and strawberry preserves in a blender, and blend until smooth.

Transfer to a glass bottle with a lid (so you can shake it later because it will separate). Store in the refrigerator for up to 7 days.

To serve, shake vigorously and pour into glasses.

>>> HIGH ALTITUDE—FOLLOW THE RECIPE AS NOTED.

>>> VEGAN—REPLACE THE MILK WITH UNSWEETENED VANILLA COCONUT MILK.

A lot of people don't know the difference between jam, jelly, and preserves. And to be honest there's not a huge difference. Preserves contain large pieces of fruit. In jam, the fruit has been pureed, but there are still some small chunks. Jelly is made from fruit juice and is more solid and harder to spread (which is why it's my least favorite). I like preserves the best, so you'll find lots of strawberry chunks here.

Makes 6 ounces (170 grams)

8 ounces (237 grams) strawberries

1/4 cup (57 grams) cane sugar

1/2 teaspoon lemon juice

Remove the stems from the strawberries, and roughly chop them.

In a medium pot, mix together the strawberries, sugar, and lemon juice, and cook over medium heat, stirring occasionally, until the sugar has dissolved.

Turn the heat to high, and boil for 1 to 2 minutes, stirring occasionally. At this stage you can mash the strawberries with your spatula if you like.

Lower the heat to medium, and simmer for about 10 minutes, stirring occasionally, until the consistency is thick.

Transfer to a glass jar and let cool to room temperature. Store in the refrigerator for up to 2 weeks.

>>> HIGH ALTITUDE—FOLLOW THE RECIPE AS NOTED.

If you want to dip biscotti, Florentines, or any other cookie in chocolate, tempering the chocolate first will give it a glossy sheen and cause it to set at room temperature without sticking to your fingers. Tempering isn't crucial to any of my recipes, but it does create better-looking cookies if you plan to give them as a gift or serve them at a dinner party. The only special equipment you need is a digital thermometer. Once you get the hang of tempering, I bet you'll start doing it all the time.

WHAT YOU'LL NEED:

Chocolate of your choice

Metal or glass bowl

Pot with water

Digital thermometer

Larger bowl filled with ice (or a bag of ice)

Choose which chocolate you'll be tempering: milk chocolate, white chocolate, or dark chocolate. Look for melting chocolates, and avoid semisweet chocolate chips, which can sometimes have additives that keep them from melting well. My favorite brand of chocolate for melting is Mama Ganache, which is easy to buy online at www.mamaganache.com.

Finely chop the chocolate, and divide it into two piles: one containing about 20% of the chocolate, and the other about 80% of the chocolate. (Eyeballing the amounts is okay.) Set aside.

To make a double boiler: Set a metal or glass bowl over a pot of simmering water, making sure the bowl does not touch the water. Place the large pile of chocolate in the bowl, and stir until it melts. Continue heating. For white chocolate, heat until it reaches 100°F. For milk chocolate, heat until it reaches 110°F. For dark chocolate, heat until it reaches 115°F.

Remove the bowl from the heat, and immediately add the small pile of chocolate, stirring vigorously until it melts and combines completely. Adding this small amount of already tempered chocolate back to the melted chocolate will help the chocolate "remember" what's it's supposed to become again. Set the bowl containing the chocolate in the larger bowl of ice or on top of a bag of ice to stop the heating process. Remove from the ice and let sit until the chocolate reaches 89°F for milk chocolate and white chocolate, or 91°F for dark chocolate. Don't let it stay on the ice or the bottom will be completely hardened.

To test whether your chocolate is properly tempered, drop a small dollop onto a piece of parchment paper, and place it in the freezer for a minute. If the chocolate looks semiglossy and stays firm when you snap it—then you did it! If it's sticky, you can start over by reheating the chocolate and adding a little more already-tempered chocolate.

At this point it's ready to be dipped into, drizzled over, or poured onto whatever you like. Be sure to refrigerate the chocolate-dipped or -drizzled food for about 1 hour, until the chocolate sets.

>>> HIGH ALTITUDE—FOLLOW THE RECIPE AS NOTED.

ACKNOWLEDGMENTS

First, I have to thank my husband, Delaney. Without his help I wouldn't have known I loved writing and creating cookbooks. He showed me InDesign and a few settings on my Nikon camera, and I've been obsessed ever since. If it weren't for him, I wouldn't have known how to put my creativity into something tangible that I could share with others. I couldn't have produced this book without him. And of course he helped taste-test everything. Love you, babe.

Clare Pelino, I am so thankful to call you my agent and friend. This book would not have been possible without you and all your hard work and persistence. We make a great team, and I love that you are as optimistic as me! I absolutely love working with you, and am so thankful that you see my vision and that you care about the food and ingredients as much as I do. We always seem to be on the same page. We did it, Clare, and I cannot wait to start the next one! Actually, we both know I'm already working on it, and this is just the first of our projects together.

Thank you Claire Schulz and Da Capo for loving my idea to write this book! I was so humbled when you told me that you had been following our small bake shop in a tiny mountain town on Instagram for so long. In that moment it seemed like fate, and I knew we would be working together. I will be forever grateful to you for giving me my first book deal.

Renée Sedliar, thank you for stepping in and filling Claire's big shoes. We are cookie soul mates, as we discovered the first week working together. There will never be enough coconut, chocolate, or ginger for me, and I'm so glad my editor feels the same way. Thank you for making this book shine in its best light.

Amy Treadwell, I feel like the luckiest author ever as I have gotten to work with not one, not two, but three amazing editors on this book! Thank you for understanding my vision and my expertise as a baker, as well as the things I truly believe are important within this book. And of course for containing all my babbling and helping me streamline my words. I can only hope that the home baker enjoys and uses this book as much as I enjoyed writing it and making it come to life with your help.

A big thank you to Michael Clark and Kelley Blewster for helping fine-tune everything once the book was written. And thank you to everyone at Da Capo who has worked behind the scenes to help make this book a reality.

Thank you Kimmy, Chris, Thea, and Matt for so much more than I can list here. Your constant support means the world to me. I couldn't ask for better friends and partners at Dessert'D Organic Bake Shop.

Thank you YiaYia for cultivating my love of cookies. Thank you Mom, Cheryl Ririe, for raising me to care about ingredients and what I eat. And, thank you Dad, Matt Kurz, for encouraging my cookie baking at all costs, and for helping me create the Dad's Coconut Chocolate Chip Cookie—you are a legend. Thanks to all my friends and family for helping me taste-test cookies all these years; you know who you are.

Last, I want to thank Heather Dreiling. Because of the chance you gave us (or one could argue didn't give us), I found a new passion. Sometimes things don't turn out exactly how you expect, but sometimes they can be better. And this book is proof of that. So, to anyone who has ever had something not work out, just believe that something else is meant to be, and you will find it.

INDEX

Note: Page references in *italics* indicate photographs.

ABOUT THE AUTHOR

MIMI COUNCIL OPENED DESSERT'D ORGANIC BAKE SHOP (then Mimi's Cookie Bar) in September 2011, and it's been growing ever since. Mimi is a self-taught baker who loves sweets just as much as she appreciates living an active and healthy lifestyle. Her recipes, which feature minimal and organic ingredients, represent the kind of lifestyle she lives. Mimi has made a name for herself by providing all of her recipes with a single quick variation to allow them to be baked at sea level or high altitude. Mimi and her desserts have been featured in *Shape* magazine and on the websites the FeedFeed, Green Wedding Shoes, 100 Layer Cake, and the Nest, among others.

MIMI LIVES AND BAKES IN MAMMOTH LAKES, CALIFORNIA.

@dessertdorganic

@mimibakescookies

www.dessertd.com

Dessert'D Organic Bake Shop

588 Old Mammoth Rd. #2

Mammoth Lakes, CA 93546